ETHICS:
A
SAVOIR
FAIRE

ETHICS: A SAVOIR FAIRE

APARNA SHARMA

PARTRIDGE
A Penguin Random House Company

To order additional copies of this book, contact
Partridge India
000 800 10062 62
orders.india@partridgepublishing.com

www.partridgepublishing.com/india

Episodes

"Dedicated to my Parents"

A Foreword

The manner in which corruption and crime is mounting day by day, in spite of various measures to curb them, it becomes mandatory to cover this passage from ethics to refined and sophisticated psychology. The book is written with a perception to send a message to the society for managing the personal and professional fronts with an ethical reminder. Not only this but with the varying pace of society ethics had been kept in backdrop and the work is an effort to sensitize people over this vicinity.

Today may be we are not realizing the value of ethics and morality, as the race is of opportunist people, but down the line a decade or may be less than that the selfish ends will be categorised and will be detected as the cancerous tentacles.

With a very slow pace, but people today started searching for aesthetic solace once again, and underway realizing this hard core truth of life, that to develop an inclination towards values and welfare state instead of selfish motive ethical sense is indispensable. So this work will be fruitful as it comes up with the reasons of this materialistic mindset and comes up with the suggestions as well to get rid of this.

The suggestions can appeal to the customary readers and to the researchers of this field as the work has taken the examples from the literature, religion, leadership, spirituality etc. From the business covetousness to the spirituality at workplace many issues of the day to day life are taken into consideration.

Book will be helpful for the human values, organizational behaviour, and ethical fields of management for the students and for the researchers as well. The common focus and closeness of the topics to aesthetic sense make it readable for the broad-spectrum readers as well.

I like to extend my thanks to my father Shri. A.N.Sharma, mother Smt. Saroj Sharma for their unending motivation and courage, my sister Shachi Sharma and my brother Shashank Sharma for their cooperation and valuable suggestions, and my beloved niece Ananya Sharma who is always willing to see my name on books. With this I like to extend my heartiest thanks to all the teachers so far, my well wishers and to all the people who gave me lessons directly or indirectly. I like to give special thanks to Dr. Ashok Shastri & to Prof. Jagdeesh Luthra who inspired me in various ways to come up with innovations. Last, but not the least, thanks to Almighty for the completion of this work.

Dr. Aparna Sharma

Chapter 1

Introduction

The world is passing through a very crucial phase, humanity needs to ponder over the passage between materialism and morality. We have travelled a long journey from Stone Age to Nanotechnology and even challenged the domain of God at times. In spite of all this we are still unable to understand the human brain which comes with unexpected positivity and negativity. The psychological disorders are there even in very well off and cultured people.

Since the inception of society, there was a time when an amalgamation of religion, morality and code of conduct emerged in name of ethics and people religiously followed that. In due course of time ethics became a relative theory and the societies diluted it as per their convenience. It is said, that the life of man is determined by his thoughts, so supervise especially your thoughts because they are the ones which determine your life. Point is, that because of all this ethics is considered to be a strict discipline, to be followed with conscious mind which includes features like perceptions, sensations, memories, feelings and fantasies etc. inside our current awareness.

Then at times it is supported by The Bhagwad Gita(III:4-8) which points out that activity is inherent in man's very nature. Sloth is simply a wrong activity.

"No man shall escape from act

By shunning actions: nay and none shall come

By mere renouncement up to perfectness.

Nay, and no jot of time, at any time,

Rests any action less, his nature's law

Compels him, even unwilling into act.

(for thought is act in fancy)

……..he who, with strong body serving mind,

Gives up his mortal powers to worthy work,

Not seeking gain, Arjuna! Such a one

Is honorable,

Do thine allotted task!"[1]

Since the inception of social structure we witness some customs and traditions which determine the code of conduct and rule of law. For ages based on those regulations the justice was imparted to people and so they became the order of the living in name of ethics which guide us to distinguish between right and wrong.

The stability of any society depends entirely on how an individual performs his prescribed duties, and when the people look towards their material gains instead of duties, it shakes. In name of professionalism we are preparing the people who when move to earnings ask about the package instead of their duties. One should work with the philosophy of life and work that too without selfishness, as the time reveals that unselfishness stands as the present age Dharma and no doubt that is ethical in nature as well.

"Where is the wisdom we have lost in knowledge?

Where is the knowledge we have lost in information?"[2]

The manner in which corruption and crime is increasing day by day, in spite of various measures it becomes mandatory to cover this passage from ethics to refined and sophisticated psychology. Unless and until the sensitivity can't be provoked we cannot think of any improvement in the mindset of people, and this task can be done by the literature and aesthetic works. It is said that unless the conscious of a person is not awake he will not turn to be a better one.

Encouraging spiritual experience and greater self-understanding enables the readers to be reflective, creative, curious and critical, can facilitate readers to build up high order skills. Spiritual growth occurs when readers respond personally to a written work of art or literature and when this becomes an aesthetic experience for the reader. Literature gives multiple scope for developing inner life of a reader with its immaterial intelligent, sentiment characteristics which can be defined as that unique attitude or frame of mind specific to each individual. Spirituality is an attitude or a way of life that recognizes something we might call the spirit. (Halfords 1998, p 28)

Spirituality no doubt is ethical, as it connects not only to self-betterment but to the betterment of the world, of nature and so on. Ethics can be linked to each and every field and its importance to all of them. In lifestyle it earns solace and peace of mind, in science it earns prosperity through innovations, in economics it earns the utilization of money for the riches and rags as well, in culture it is deep rooted, in politics it governs without biases, in service it serves more, and in day to day life it makes one courageous to face all ills and to manage everything. What more to say, it is an essential need to live life.

In vivid fields, it is observed that the people these days are becoming too professional. At times it comes to the cost of ethics. Medical line compromising over correct diagnose and remedy, political line over ideology, administration over luxury and leisure, police over making money, teachers and scholars over borrowed ideas, social workers over page 3 coverage, corporate and economists over exploitation, and so on.......

The moral or ethical point of view involves impartiality regarding the interests of all, including oneself. It involves abstracting from one's own interests and one's particular attachment to others. To be moral is to have cultural sensitivity, to respect others as having equal value to oneself, and as having an equal right to pursue their own interests. One acts contrary to morality in preferring one's own interests, or the interests of those whom one likes and is connected to, simply because they are one's own or one's friend's' interests. Moral principles must be universal or universalizable. They must be valid for all and compelling to any rational moral agent.

Ethics must involve self-control. It cannot depend on our own interests, desires, emotions or attachments, but has to depend on rationality and logic of public welfare. The concept of moral bears the heritage of different moral traditions from which it gathers different sorts of meanings[3].

Many perceptions stand with that ethics is a relative property, the one which is moral for me may be not for someone else. Still one thing which remains attached to it is that some where the feeling of wellbeing and welfare is there. It can be of self, of community, of nation or of humanity on the whole, but it is there.

The need to have a discussion over the concept of ethics is felt as the societal norms are at stake. Selfishness overpowered the virtues of mankind. The rat race of power and pelf has shaken the deep rooted foundations of welfare of all thinking. Wellbeing, relations, sanctity, altruism, concern, compassion etc. are left much behind in that race. As a result selfishness, and use and throw psychology appears all around, which needs to be checked and curtailed as well.

Relationships are used as a medium to fulfill expectations instead of expressing happiness and feeling of joyfulness. If we make our life an expression of joy with values and not in pursuit of happiness then relationships naturally become wonderful where your needs are gone and happiness is on self start, you are then prepared to hold infinite beautiful relationships.

The goal of ethics is to make its follower a better person by establishing in him unshakable virtues and values.

Religion and spirituality is there to institute that as none of them differ in their value system. The difference lies in the instrument of application. To create an upbeat future for our planet we must learn to expand our span of ethical control to cover as many levels of the consciousness as possible.

Philip Mercer claims that concern and sympathy for a suffering person involve being disposed to do something about the person's condition[4]. It means that the prosperity of all is the ultimate aim of ethics, by removing negativity and inculcating positivity. This is only possible by the efforts of ethical bent of mind. That is why today we need this as the world is full of criticism, hatred, communalism, ill will, and use and throw psychology as well. Somewhere or the other a start is not only required but the dire need of circumstances. In order to sustain mankind and this world as well ethics are the most essential traits of an individual.

References:

1. Yogananda Paramahansa, *Autobiography of a Yogi,* Yogoda Satsang Society of India, Kolkata, 2011

2. Eliot T, *Religion & Literature: In Selected Essays*, London, Faber, 1935

3. MacIntyre, Alasdair, A Short History of Ethics, NewYork Macmillan, 1966

4. Iris Murdoch, *The Sovereignty of Good*, New York, Shocken, 1971.

Chapter 2

Work Mechanism &
Diverse Perspectives

Watch your thoughts; they become words.

Watch your words; they become actions.

Watch your actions; they become character.

Watch your character; it becomes your destiny. – Frank Outlaw

The other day I was going through the autobiography of APJ Kalam, in which he illuminated about his native place Rameshwaram, and the family- middle lower class. How he had to move out for studies, his destiny was to remain a fisherman if he wanted a peaceful life. But his innovation to be a scientist and that too with full dedication put him on the ladder of success from Rocket launching to the prestige of President of India. Throughout his narration there had been the importance of integrative discerning.

The interdisciplinary approach is the trend of the day. This requires the comprehensive dealing which is only possible through integrative thinking. Human brain is having extensive potential, if given the right direction it can result in lot of positive outcome. The studies show that thinking over one particular issue with different perspectives brings out the best results. To confine we can say that when the sensitivity of heart (mind) is combined with the analytical and practical approach of mind integrative philosophy surfaces there.

In the globalized era one has to ponder over this issue. When the geographical boundaries are merging and collaborating for future perspective we should also take collective approach for the advancement of humanity and human beings in personal as well. Interdependency is a known feature of society, which proves that for a successful life one has to touch every aspect of life. Why in Indian philosophy the family life (Grahast Ashram) is considered the best? The answer is; it tests the multidimensionality of the individual.

The focus is on, how integrative thinking with ethical perspective becomes the power of mind and helps the one to pass the critical tests of life. Integration is the art of living and letting live. The relation between law of nature and integrative thinking can be seen everywhere, the politicians, administrators, literary laureates, scientists, economists, scholars, students, housewives, classes as well as masses, who so ever is doing best in its respective field is likely to practice integrative thinking. It enhances the potential with this power and can contribute to the society as well. For creating wonders in materialistic world we need the serenity of nature too.

Life is like a tough field of battle, full of adverse forces. In order to combat the obstacles of path we have to make sure that all the adverse forces have to be tackled with vision and strategy. For that very purpose we need a systematic direction given to our thinking in an integrative manner. Thinking is a natural[1] process which no one can escape, and integrative thinking is an extended version of it to bring out over all positive results for prosperity. In the course of their existence all people have experiences, and respond to the roots and traditions of their culture, spirituality and the social, political, and economic conditions in which they find themselves.[2] The observance shows that in every era there is need to touch all the aspects and fields of society as they are the part and parcel of life and contributes to success and prosperity. Whether we talk of an individual or we go to the level of Nation or even beyond that it can be easily seen that nothing could be left out due to interdependency in every walk of life.

This proves that the power of mind lies in integration only. Take a simple example, 'Democracy' which is termed as the civilized mandate to run the system needs to be impartial in terms of caste, colour, creed, financial status, qualifications etc. to work for the egalitarian concept. No doubt this to be followed requires the assimilation of integrities and ideas i.e. integrative approach.

The need to discuss this here is that there is a misconception that thinking is a job of philosophers and no one else should poke his nose in this domain. But the fact is that the key position holder and a lay man of daily wages need to think for making both the ends meet, the only difference is that of philosophical thinking. One is meant for a confined group and for short term goal, and the other is for the human race and meant for the long term goals. In order to achieve positive and concrete results one has to go for the productive aspect of thinking as it is a way to shine a bright light on the potential connections that are waiting to be discovered all around us. To create the future, one has to be able to imagine it. It is a disciplinary approach to ruminate more creatively and effectively[3].

The emphasis should be on right training to think better. The more one practice the better he will get, resulting in more opportunities to make a better world, a better organization resulting in a better life. For the right training, one has to think with the union of heart and mind. Unless one decorate the intellect with the emotions the solid outcome is impossible. Emotions organize intellectual capacities and indeed create the sense of self.[4]

The era is of Globalization, which varies from the expansion of cultural influences across borders to the enlargement of economic and business relations throughout the world. It is through global movement of ideas, people, goods and technology that different regions of the world have tended in general to the benefit from the progress and development occurring interwovenly.[5] With perfect leadership irrespective of East or West, communalism or terrorism, cultural or scientific, developed or under developed everywhere the solution to gaudy problems is possible through integrative acuity. Integrative thinkers work to see the whole problem, embrace its multi varied nature and understands the complexity of its casual relationships. They work to shape and order what others see as a chaotic landscape. They search for creative resolutions to the problems typically seen by others as a simple 'fork in the road' or an irresponsible bind brought about by competing organizational interests.[6]

Making the solution through this choice is an indication of, some creativity in progress for the bright future perspectives. The live examples are there in records of history in name of various revolutions like French, Russian, Industrial, Renaissance, Indian Independence and many more. The above mentioned goals were achieved, because the integrative approach was applied. It is said that the world cannot run on gun point, rather the solutions can be there where we judge and solve the problem by considering both the sides of the coin. Assimilation of ideas for bringing out the best possible way is the need of hour.

The Salience, Causality, Sequencing & Resolution, the 4 steps[7] according to choice cascade model are the mandatory units of success, even if followed in the reversible direction. Success is something in which you find meaning of your life, your goal. If one knows the 'why' of existence he may find 'how' also. One who finds the meaning of this why & how is successful and content. In order to search for this we have to contemplate and practice multidimensionality. This is the only power of mind which is essential for leading a milestone making life.

Power of mind is not only a term; it is an experimentation of virtues and caliber, their testament and then implementation. In order to be unique one has to follow the saying of Swami Vivekananda, 'strength is life, weakness is death', i.e. to live a life one has to overcome the barriers and obstacles through will power and mind power. An example: the people suffering with severe diseases are treated physically as well as psychologically so that they should integrate and assimilate their thoughts, think positive to fight with adversities and should think for a bright future, and this is the power of mind. The plans should be a combination of continuity, diligent hard work and perseverance, and religiously strived for fruitful result.

Pondering over problems beyond a certain point is certain to create confusion and worry. There comes a time when any more investigation and thinking is harmful. There comes a time when we must decide and act and never lookback.[8] The turbulent billows of the fretful surface leave the deep parts of the ocean undisturbed, and to him who has a hold on vaster and more permanent realities, the hourly vicissitudes of his personal destiny seem relatively insignificant things. The really religious person is accordingly unshakable and full of equanimity, and calmly ready for any duty that the day may bring forth[9] the integrative thinking of the background is responsible for this.

What more to say even the law of nature and the perception of our historians defends this rule, it is said that traditional Indian values must be viewed both from the angle of the individual and from that of geographically delimited agglomeration of people or groups enjoying a common system of leadership which we call the state. The Indian state's special feature is the peaceful or perhaps the most peaceful, coexistence of the social groups of various historical provenances which mutually adhere in a geographical, economic and political sense, without ever assimilating to each other in social terms, in ways of thinking or even in language[10]. Thus the role of integrative thinking is there since ages for all the fields of life, when revolution was required then it emerged out as Bhagat Singh, when strategic attack was needed it was in Gandhi. When some concrete result is the requirement then we need productiveness as it is specifically for those times when you need new ideas to address challenges[11]. If we really want to create a high performance organization, department or team planning and implementation must fit and work together as a system (result of integrative thinking). The word system is made up of a set of components that work together for the overall objective of the whole output[12].

Integration of body, mind, heart, and spirit is the power by which all set ambitions can be fulfilled. A deep thought can make it clear that in absence of collective approach no one can work out for the attainment of success; that collective approach is nothing but the power of mind. Mind plays an important role in fulfilling our desires. To focus on mind power, first we have to think what exactly we want to get or wish to do. But this is not very simple rather requires deep thinking, investigation and time which is utilizing the power of mind, as thoughts possess power[13].

In order to make changes in life we have to make changes in thinking process to make a change in our behaviour, actions, attitude and then results. Thoughts are the part and parcel of our subconscious mind; keep on affecting our lives, atmosphere and the society we belong to. Since ages of Ashoka to the era of Obama the power of diversified thoughts are seen, it is only the thoughts that rule the world no matter which the time period is or who the personality is, the names which are to be written in golden words as a record are nothing but the outcome of systematic approach towards positive strategic and integrative thinking. This works to solve business problems, clarify situations, develop technical solutions, suggests new products, reduce conflicts, map strategies, enhance relationships, reduce frustrations, orient careers, and resolve personal dilemmae[14].

In society admiration is there for the people who are keeping a balance of materialism and spiritualism in their life, who work on a deeper level of thinking – a paradigm based on the principles that accurately describe the territory of effective human being and interacting to solve the deep concerns of life. Philosopher Herb Shepherd describes the healthy balanced life around four values; perspective (spiritual), autonomy (mental), connectedness (social), and tone (physical)these values can be seen as essential and interrelated part of life and only integrative thinking is there behind the attainment of these four values[15],

1. Physical; exercise, nutrition, stress management

2. Social/ emotional; service, empathy, synergy, intrinsic security

3. Spiritual; value clarification & commitment, study, meditation

4. Mental; reading, visualizing, planning, writing

Though the integrative thinking is not a necessary condition for success[16] but still best minds use it to find profitable and innovative resolutions to seemingly irresolvable conflicts. It is practiced by leaders who have the predisposition and the capacity to hold two diametrically opposing ideas in their heads; they are able to produce a synthesis that is superior to either of opposing idea[17].

Your thoughts, which are part of your mind, possess power. The thoughts that you most often think tend to come true. If you pour your mental energy into the same thoughts or mental images day after day, they will become stronger and stronger, and would consequently affect your attitude, expectations, behavior and actions. These thoughts and mental images can even be subconsciously perceived by other people, who would then offer you help or opportunities. Your thoughts can also create what is usually termed as coincidence. They can attract into your life corresponding events, situations and opportunities. The life is full of problems today in our haste to learn and teach Problem solving skill (PSK) we forgot to nurture Problem preventing values (PPV)[18], the need of time is to nurture the art of integrative thinking. This requires the DTC method of discipline, thought and control introduced by Frank R. Wallace in The Advanced Concepts of Poker[19] to perform actions that increase the bottom line, an intense focusing of one's brain is required.

The brain is naturally tuned to point out what is wrong and what is right. Then the creativity and modifications are required i.e. provocations and movements to produce new ideas. After this a control and check is also necessary for management of thinking process.[20] One can go for various methods of keeping a check on thinking like the company of good people, going through good literature, practicing exercises and meditation etc. this will enhance the overall caliber.

The poetic lines are,

There is no time to lose, cash your dreams before they slip away,

Dying all the time, lose your dreams, & you will lose your mind[21].

In each strata of life the show is running because mind is there, in absence of thoughts (dreams) nothing is possible. It was only a thought, years back, to land on moon which turned to reality. This was possible because of creativity only, which is an important aspect like food for mind. The essential characteristics[22] for creative decisions are strong emotions, artistic approach, boldness, innovative solutions and a need to be different. These are the features inculcated in one only through integration of thoughts.

Everywhere there is a clarion call for quiet firm and balanced people; it can be easily nurtured to the young minds if we give them the roots of culture and tradition and the wings of innovations. Integration works for centering our lives on correct principles and creating a balanced focus between doing and increasing our ability to do, we become empowered in the task of creating effective, useful, and peaceful lives… for ourselves and for our posterity[23]. This way it can be said that the power of mind is utilized. Integrative thinking is an art followed through analysis, judgment, argument, criticism and then result, with the equal participation of mind and heart. It's that skill of thinking that determines the happiness, success and prosperity in life for family as a unit and for the whole world too.

Those who value integrative thinking comprehend the nectar and become a cesspool and conglomeration of success; they easily overcome the extreme rigidities of life, piercing all darkness. Integrative thinking is an art; thinker develops a stance that embraces not fears the essential qualities of enigmatic choices. Thinker is a relentless learner who seeks to develop the repertoire of skill that enables him or her to engage the tensions between opposites long enough to transcend the duality and seek out novel solutions. They understand that they are engaged in creative process that avoids easy, pat, or formulaic answers. In fine, Integrative thinking is the management style we need if we have to solve the enigmatic problems that face our organizations in the new millennium[24]. It gives an opportunity to explore the world from different dimensions which favours the philosophy "We must not cease from exploration. And the end of all our exploring will be to arrive where we began and to know the place for the first time"[25].

Now the point is, what is the role of ethics in integrated thinking? How integration can be related to the ethical concept? Assimilation of ideas can be negative as well as positive, now at that moment the role of ethics comes, the purity of mind and the welfare of mankind are the areas which can create wonders, these days people do work with integrated concept but for the welfare of their own and to curb the progress line of others or to harm someone.

From political lanes to corporate life, form public to private everywhere the scene is same. We need to have a management which is there for the prosperity of society not for the unit only.

Since the inception of society and human beings some or the other things are there to administer. Primitive man to the machine one (robot) leadership and management remained the need. From systematic operations of the surroundings to the courage, to go with innovations according to the need; one can observe the role of management and leadership in life. The emphasis is on, that how these are directly proportional and goes hand in hand with each other.

The importance of management and leadership in day to day life makes us ponder, that a person breaking stones on the road side and the 1st man of the nation are having a good contrasting career, but the role of leadership and management is there for both of them, and not even a single day can pass in its absence. It is said that leaders are born and management could be learnt by all. Leadership is a trait of personality and management is taught as a skill. At times both appear quiet different and sometime interdependent. This way it could be said that both are having almost equal weight age in terms of individuality. The prime focus is on how ethical leadership results in good management and how the ethical management is surety of good leadership.

The competitive society which accepts the theory of the survival of the fittest needs to be skilled in some traits. In this specific zone leadership and management traits come first. It appears as if the two are directly proportional to each other. A set up where discipline is maintained and system runs smoothly is example of good management and when this discipline under various categories is carried outside that system to make the mile stone then it is leadership. The appreciation of the tasks done by people is the example of good management, and if people try to follow one's footsteps or wish to keep the torch lighted by one that proves the leadership caliber of the person, as the essence of leadership is followership.[26]

It is said that the concept of management emerged in 20th century[27].The study of management as a discipline might be new but then the fact is that it has been there since ages. When kingship was the order of the day the positions were the examples of leadership and the work done under them was the example of management.

Management consists of helping people set ambitious yet realistic goals and motivating them towards the achievement of those goals. Since people began forming groups to accomplish aims they could not achieve as individuals, managing has been essential to ensure the coordination of individual efforts[28]. Now it is convenient to divide managerial functions as planning, organizing, staffing, leading and controlling[29]. Certain features of organization such as hierarchal arrangement, loyalty, obedience, controlled entrances, intelligent secrecy, recognition devices, when used astutely bring forth more powerful associations of human beings and enable clusters to move towards objectives with greater smoothness and efficiency. This important instrument of leadership stands throughout history as a fundamental aspect of living.[30]

When one is ready to face the past without regret, handle the present with confidence and prepare for the future without fear true leadership is there. On the same track in terms of management one who learns to rectify the mistakes of past, look for simple solutions, enjoys every little moment of present and keeps a vision for prosperous tomorrow is a good manager. Leadership is a rage of emotions which pampers to do something new i.e. known for some uniqueness, it can go to any extent. Management is doing the same things done by the ancestors but in a different manner i.e. earn appreciation for style. It is about setting things right and devising a new eclectic way of life. Warren Bennis summarized the differences among two as[31]

1. The manager administers, the leader innovates.

2. The manager is a copy; the leader is an original.

3. The manager focuses on systems and structures; the leader focuses on people.

4. The manager relies on control; the leader inspires trust.

5. The manager has a short range view; the leader has a long range perspective.

6. The manager asks how and when; the leader what and why.

7. The manager has his eyes always on the bottom line; the leader has his eyes on the horizon.

8. The manager imitates; the leader originates.

9. The manager accepts the status quo, the leader challenges it.

10. The manager is the classic good soldier; the leader is his own person.

11. The manager does things right; the leader does the right thing.

The description is quite interesting and authentic but today the focus is on how in spite of the differences these can go hand in hand for the concept of managerial leadership.

There is a renewed call today for charismatic leaders in organizations. There is also increasing concern today about narcissistic propensities vitiating leadership roles in various institutions. There is an increasing talk now on visionary abilities, on character, on heroism, in leadership roles. All the Rajarshi type leaders in India's history had been constructively charismatic, visionary heroic, and were free from the bane of narcissism. Why? Because, they were close to truth as joy. Studies of their lives reveal two mutually consistent, abiding endeavours; Self-control and renunciation.[32]. This proves that leadership does not begin only with vision, but with getting people to confront the brutal facts and to act on the implications.

This shows that since the inception of civilization we are having enormous images of leadership and management. Now coming to the interdependency between leadership and management we can follow up with the concept of good to great i.e. good management leads to great leadership. In this stream leaders never wanted to become larger than life heroes. They never aspired to be put on a pedestal or become unreachable icons. They were seemingly ordinary people quietly producing extraordinary results.[33]

Within the strands of managing, leaders are, the outcome as 'leaders don't do different things, they do the things differently'. To make the people workout in the adverse circumstances is a feature of collective approach of leadership and management. Instead of firing honest and able people who are not performing well, it is important to try to move them once or twice or thrice or three times to other positions where they might blossom[34]. True leaders help to attain objectives through the maximum application and utilization of capabilities.

A culture of discipline involves duality. On one hand it requires people to adhere to a consistent system; yet on the other hand it gives them freedom and responsibility within the frame work of that system[35].We can say that leadership and management are going hand in hand when it works for preserving the core values and core purpose and bringing change to the cultural and operating practices and also trying to alter specific goals and strategies. In true sense only then the fragrance of innovations with antique and aesthetic touch could be felt.

Leadership has an extraordinary power, but it has been advised to leaders that they may not treat princes as princes but they should treat persons as persons[36]. It can make the difference between success and failure in any thing you do for yourself or for any group to which you belong[37]. For solving of any problem leaders work with three tools of: brainstorming, psychological techniques, and analysis of alternatives[38].

Leadership and management both works for some identification and in the long run contribute to the nationalism also. The sense of identity leaves the issue of appropriate actions and policies entirely open to scrutiny and choice. This applies to the science and technology on the one hand and to economic, social and cultural on the other[39]. It can be said that management is a skill by which we generally make people work for a specific job in a systematic manner. The art of getting what one wants and making people like it not only stimulates imagination, intellectual faculties, intuitive impulses, and insatiable appetites but also offers challenges to leaders and compensations to followers and institutions[40].

In the changing scenario, the need of hour is that one should apply the amalgamation of both these traits, as today society doesn't require dictatorial leaders to enforce their version but requires the collective managerial leadership (inclusive of strategic, transactional, visionary, charismatic, empowering, moral, sevent, entrepreneurial, and innovative leadership) for maintaining ourselves in the globalized culture of world. It can be easily noticed that when managers are involved in influencing a group to meet its goals, they are involved in leadership. When leaders are involved in planning, organizing, staffing, and controlling, they are involved in management[41]. At various levels the role of leaders and managers comes out on similar parameters as they overlap in practical terms. Inspiration by a leader often plays a major role in spurring people on to maximum performance, not only this but the second stage of performance management is encouragement[42].

The secret of life lies in honesty and bravery, numbers do not count, nor does wealth or poverty, a handful of men can throw the world off its hinges, provided they are united in thought, word and deed[43]. The relevance of these details can be observed in life, time to time when we say, teach yourselves, teach everyone his real nature, call upon the sleeping soul and see how it awakes. Power will come, glory will come, goodness will come, purity will come and everything that is excellent will come when the sleeping soul is roused to self-conscious activity[44]. These applications are very well required in the materialistic world of today to make the balance. The communication gap needs to be removed from every level and every minor suggestion has to be kept in consideration if it is worthwhile. These are the only basics if dealt within the circle of leadership and management, it can create wonders and sure positive outcome can be seen from the level of individual to the level of nation and finally to the universe too.

This discourse is not to be viewed as a mere academic product but as an expression of many sided activities of society/s growth. A person may have all the traits of a leader, but if he/she doesn't personally see to the development of new leaders the organization won't be sustainable[45] In fine the role of management is inevitable.

From the economic growth to cultural fusion, individual's success to nation's strength, materialism to spirituality i.e. all the contrasting as well as the parallel stages can run smoothly and successfully when charged with proper management under approachable leadership. In fine a combination of Management and Leadership says, once you solve the problems of man to your own satisfaction, you had your philosophy of life and evolved your own art of living. All this you must apply to the present situation and out of it will arise a new creation and not a mere repetition, a creation which the soul of your people will own for itself and proudly offer to the world as its tribute to the welfare of man[46].

The word Ethics sounds amusing in the world of materialism, where the people are not having any concern for the idealistic life. Money is all that matters. In this scenario we need the leaders with ethical bent of mind. But the question is can we call our leaders of today as leaders? In majority the answer is 'No'. The reason behind this 'no' is that somewhere they are not satisfying our expectation of ideology. We are not finding that as if they are working for our cause. The reason in the background is the lack of ethics.

Since ages the leaders of all fields are considered to be the perfect and sensitive people who can fight for another's cause, and the one who is ethical can do it best. Rather we can say that leadership and ethics go hand in hand. One can feel to fight for justice only then when values are there. This lesson of life starts at an early stage of upbringing and the outcome is welfare of the society.

Globalization has poured too much of competition among the human beings. Every person is craving to be the best. In this cut throat competition people are engaging into unethical practices and have become too much materialistic. Players in the Global industry are aiming to prove themselves and to achieve their high set goals; and for this they require high quality of ethical leadership, who can guide them towards their goals. However in the era of NANO technology, the word ethics is decorating the idealistic articles and books only; it brings amusement to the faces and a person who speaks about ethics is considered to be outdated or below standard. The ones who talk about ethics are themselves unethical often. In this crucial phase where people are craving for ethical leadership, it is very important to ponder over the relevance of ethics in life and then in leadership.

The Latin word 'ethicus' and the Greek word 'ethikos' from which the word ethics has been derived means character or manners[47]. It tends to define how individuals choose to interact with one another. It can be extended to imply systematizing, defending and recommending concepts of right and wrong behaviour. In philosophy, ethics define what is good for the individual and for society and ratifies the nature of duties that people owe to themselves and to one another. Ethics is thus said to be the science of moral, moral principles and recognized rules of conduct. Ethics are the values inculcated to our conscious and latent mind, both from the time of our understanding to the outer world. Philosophers viewed ethics as a system of moral principles and the methods for applying them. It deals with values relating to human conduct with respect to the right and wrong of certain actions and to the goodness and badness of the motives and ends of such actions.

Ethics is a subject that deals with human beings. Humans by their nature are capable of judging between right and wrong, good and bad. It is a normative science, i.e. a guide or control of action; so, normative ethics tells us what we ought to do and what not to do. Its objective is to set a standard code for the moral behaviour and make recommendations about the desired behaviour.

On the other hand Leadership has been described as the process of social influence in which one person can enlist the aid and support of others in the accomplishment of a common task. It is ultimately about creating a way for people to contribute to make something extraordinary happen. It involves authority and responsibility in terms of deciding the way ahead and being held responsible for the success or failure in achieving the agreed objectives. It involves the application of certain values. Leadership based on moral principles requires that followers be given enough knowledge of alternatives to make intelligent choices when it comes to responding to a leader's proposal.

Leadership values can be classified as[48];

Ethical virtues: old fashioned character tests such as sobriety, chastity, abstention, kindness, altruism and other;

"Ten commandments" rules of personal conduct such as honesty, integrity, trustworthiness, reliability, reciprocity, accountability;

Moral values such as, security, liberty, equality, justice, community (brother hood and sisterhood) etc.

Leadership is all about resolving paradoxes and crises[49] in the absence of clear knowledge on where to draw a line. Great leaders try to anticipate changes they encourage group members not to use the best practices of others as benchmarks but to find innovative solutions so that others will use their practices as their own benchmarks. Leaders know what they value. They also recognize the importance of ethical behaviour. The best leaders exhibit both their values and their ethics in their leadership style and actions. In leadership ethics and values should be visible. As a leader, one should choose the values and the ethics that are most important, the values and ethics one believes, in defining an individual's character. One has to live them visibly every day at work. Living values is one of the most powerful tools available to help one lead and influence others.

Ethical values are crucially important to leaders whether in politics, education or other fields. A question emerges, 'Why there is a need for ethics'? Are the people unable to carry on their tasks without ethics? No, it is not so, rather the ethics impart us the confidence as normative theory says that ethics is righteous and resulting good. It could be said that ethics form the base of a lifestyle and ultimately provides firm and reputed status in society. So it is an essential feature of leadership as leaders are always respected for their positive reputation. Since ages to the modern society, if there is a mention of leaders, ethical values remain common. Even if the leaders involve in wrong practices for a while they were having ground to make it just. From Gautam Buddha, Ashoka, Akbar to Mahatma Gandhi, Chandrashekhar Azad, Rajeev Gandhi and so on......ample examples are there with an inseparable combination of ethical leadership. The value of ethics in leadership itself becomes clear when at a very small level it is there. Like in a class room, a teacher could be termed as leader and he/she has to be ethical to lead, only then the students follow their command.

Adherence to values and principles is an essential feature of traits of leadership. Moral leadership is based on the reality that we cannot violate these natural laws with impunity. These have been proved effective throughout centuries of human history. Individuals are more effective and organizations more empowered when they are guided and governed by these proven principles. These laws are not easy, quick fix solutions to personal and interpersonal problems. Rather these are foundational principles that if applied consistently become behavioural habits enabling fundamental transformations of individuals, relationships and organizations[50].

The authors of moral intelligence describe the importance of moral intelligence [51]as: "Moral intelligence directs our other forms of intelligence to do something worthwhile. Moral intelligence gives the life a purpose. Without moral intelligence, one would be able to do things and experience events, but they would lack meaning." And they promise: "the more one develop moral intelligence, the more positive changes he/ she will notice, not only in work but in personal well-being too." Staying true to moral compass will not eliminate life's inevitable conflicts. The evidence is clear – moral intelligence plays a major role in overall success. The authors of Moral Intelligence believe that good morality and high performance do not come together just by accident. They claim that successful leaders always attribute their accomplishments to a combination of their business savvy and their adherence to a moral code[52].

The need for leadership was never so great. A chronic crisis, that is, the pervasive incapacity of organizations to cope with the expectations of their constituents is now an overwhelming factor worldwide. The new leader is one who commits people to action who converts followers to leaders and who may convert leaders into agents of change. To survive in this world one needs to gain success in all the aspects of life. It is not necessary for everyone to have the traits of leadership but then they are essential for materialistic success. In order to achieve desired place in society and to make our dreams come true a combination of leadership and ethics is must. Rather it could be said that leadership with ethical bent of mind is the clarion call for today's world. One needs a balance of materialism and solace in life. Leadership traits are fulfilling the material aspect and ethics are responsible for solace in life.

Some important characteristic features of leadership are; a leader must have followers[53], there must be working relationship between the leader and his followers, the leader by his personal conduct must set an ideal before his followers, there must be community of interests between the leader and his team workers.

In modern concept the leader attempts to draw out the best in his followers by training them to share the leadership with them. Leadership is a dynamic process. Its important functions are to guide and motivate the behaviour of subordinates in furtherance of the objectives of the organization, to understand the feelings of the subordinates and their problems as the plans are translated into action.

No two individuals behave in the same manner. They have different values and personality variables and rather various moderating variables like individual characteristics, structural design of organization, the culture of workplace. And the intensity of ethical issue determines that whether a person will act in an ethical or unethical manner. But then this is the case of general masses or managers not of leaders. Leaders are supposed to be ethical and if they have to go unethical as per the rules of organization then also they have to lead the revolutionary side of the employees/ subordinates to fight against the injustice of the workplace. It is very clear that a logical and ethical reason is always there with the class of leaders, rests of the people are managers who by some means or the other manage the internal and external tasks.

Gandhi and Tagore, two types entirely different from each other and yet both of them typical of India, both in the long line of India's great men......it is not so much because of any single virtue but because of the tout ensemble, that is felt that among the world's great man today. Gandhi and Tagore were supreme as human beings. That means that the personalities can differ but their emergence as a leader, their potential of having followers needs a simple and ethical way out to deal up with major and minor issues of the day to day life. It could be said then, that to be a leader one needs to go with ethical / righteous lifestyle.

With leadership goes power like; legitimate power comes from the authority in the organization, expert power is the power of knowledge and skill, charismatic power is the power attraction or devotion, reward power i.e. the ability to reward worthy behavior and performance, coercive power is the ability to threaten or punish. Wise leadership uses power in the best interest of the people related to it. Power comes by virtue of what we are and do, and every great leader is a silent but eloquent witness to the fact that his power is derived from his devotion, his loyalty and his helpfulness to his followers in a common and important cause. Leadership is an influence, interaction process between the leader and his group of followers / subordinates. Leadership is an interpersonal and a social process. The one who happens to hold the sway over some of the attitudes, actions and behaviour of a set of people compromise his constituency.

Bhagawat Gita states that, "the one who controls the senses by the trained and purified mind and intellect, and engages the organs of action to selfless service is considered superior"[54], i.e. moral leadership is powerful and it can work wonders. Leadership has a moral component that is centrally important to all other aspects of life, because few people will trust a leader who has lied, embezzled, or hurt others. It has its roots deep within a person's belief and value structures. It begins with a powerful vision which is necessary to sustain leadership effectiveness. A vision that sets the leader on fire distinguishes that person from the followers. Leadership is characterized by the ability to bring out significant change in vision, strategy and culture as well as promote innovation in products and technologies.

Ethics has a province of its own, yet it is not entirely divorced from all other departments of study. It has indirectly to treat the several problems which are psychological, philosophical, sociological and political in nature. The psychological problems with which ethics is concerned are those of the nature of voluntary actions, classification of the springs of actions and the relation between desire and pleasure. The philosophical problems are those of essential nature of human personality, the freedom of the will, immortality of the soul, existence and perfection of God, and the moral government of the universe. The sociological problem is that of the relation of the individual to the society. The political problem is that of the relation of the individual to the state, of the ethical basis and moral functions of the state, and of international morality.

To handle these problems we need people with ethical leadership, so that the various phases of life could witness prosperity in society. Leadership is the quality of a person which can transform an ordinary to an extraordinary. This quality is must for any field of life, whether it is a battlefield, playground, business establishment or a college students association and home(on unit basis).

Though ethics is not a practical science[55], it deduces concrete duties and virtues from the notion of the Supreme good, which may guide us in the regulation of our conduct. Ethics is theory of morality. It converts moral faith into a rational vision. It criticizes the common notions of morality and discovers the rational and essential elements in them. In the present scenario there is need of rational perspective.

Ethics indirectly exert a paramount influence on all departments of our practical life. The right solution of the vital problems of religion, politics, economics, legislature, education etc. depends upon the correct notions of right or wrong. Religion must have foundations in ethics. Divorced from morality, it degenerates into superstitious blind belief in superhuman power, black magic and the like. Politics should be molded by ethics. Might should be based upon right and immoral laws should be abolished. Laws should be enacted for the improvement of the moral wellbeing of the people. Economics should be based on ethics. Production, distribution and consumption of wealth could be based on justice and equity. In education ethics is to decide what impulse and disposition in children should be strengthened and what should be suppressed. Ethics should embrace all departments of human action, exert an elevation influence upon, and raise humanity to higher level.

No doubt, to find such a sublime society the need of man power is there to implement those ethical values and concepts. In direct sense this could be said as the need of true leaders to complement their own workplace, and to lay the foundation stones of jovial world, freed of the personal, professional and social vices like greed, fear, dishonesty, suppression, terrorism, castism and elevate humanism. In fine it could be said that ethical leadership is the need of hour, the only remedy to curb the mere materialism mentality and to initiate the concept of ethical world.

Management is an inseparable discipline, and is actually an enduring part of system. Our Ancient system is famous for its vindicated perspective or rather the ethical concept was that much deep that nobody bothered to think about perforation[56]. Though we cannot deny the presence of vices, as these comes from human psychology but we can surely say that in earlier times it was quite easy to solve the related problems as the managing system was ethical.

The present modern world is doing multi-dimensional progress but still people are missing the serenity within. The time is to ponder what actually we chase for, is it the money, luxury, power…….or something else? What is lacking and where? Why today, in order to sleep, one has to take support of medicines? The answer is: the ethical note is missing from our life. These religious epics are considered as to be recited for the blessings of God, it's not only the recitation but the follow-up of wisdom given in them that could fetch the tranquility back. There is a need to revive these lessons and to benefit from them.

We focus on various aspects of management in Ramayana & how to read between the lines, the methods through which one can get into the ethical management, which can liberate the tensions up to an extent, and with fast material steps would be able to spend a contended life.

Globalization has decanted too much of competition among the human beings. Every person is craving for the best.

Unethical practices are being resorted to in this era of cut throat competition and people have become too much materialistic. All players in the Global industry are aiming to prove themselves and to achieve their high set goals; and for this they require high quality of ethical management and leadership, which can guide them towards their goals.

Management has been described as a social process involving responsibility for effective economic planning & regulation of operation of an enterprise in the fulfilment of cherished purposes[57]. It is a dynamic process consisting of various elements and activities which are different from operative functions like marketing, finance, purchase etc. Rather these activities are common to each and every manger irrespective of his level or status.

Different experts have classified functions of management. According to George & Jerry, "There are four fundamental functions of management i.e. planning, organizing, actuating and controlling." According to Henry Fayol, "To manage is to forecast and plan, to organize, to command, & to control."[58]

The famous Epic Ramayana, provides with its religious sanctity a base for the incorporation of ethical management which is the need of hour. The storyline of the epic tells us about the refined manner in which various planning, organizing, staffing, directing and controlling decisions of today could be taken in consideration of its characters. It gives a glimpse of the system where there is no infraction of the rules.

The Ramayana is a much more focused story with fewer characters. Lord Rama conveyed mainly through his actions thus drawing upon the insights which individuals and the organizations can use to grow and prosper. An attempt has been made to assimilate the spirit of this epic for application in the field of daily management practice and in the wider arena of creating better individuals and in turn better corporates.

To the north of the Ganga was the great kingdom Kosala, made fertile by the river Sarayu. Its capital was Ayodhya, built by Manu, the famous ruler of the Solar dynasty. King Dasaratha ruled the kingdom from the capital city of Ayodhya. The people of Kosal were happy, contented and virtuous.

Having firm faith in system indicates the ethical management of kingdom, king Dashratha planned to coronate his eldest son Rama, to carry out the administration, as his successor. He was reminded of a solemn promise made by him to Kaikayi years back and just for keeping his words (considered as oral law of those times) gave exile to his son Rama. Lord Rama a static and dynamic leader accepted exile without any objection, with the concept that the state can never take a wrong decision. Bharat the younger brother of Rama ruled Ayodhaya for 14 years, managed everything and then returned the empire to Rama on his way back to Ayodhaya.[59]

Planning is a systematic thinking about ways & means for accomplishment of pre-determined goals. Planning is necessary to ensure proper utilization of resources - human & non-human. It is all pervasive; an intellectual activity and also helps in avoiding confusion, uncertainties, risks, wastages etc[60].

The plot of Ramayana provides a planned approach in order to get systematic commencement of the work. When Kaikayi asked for the promised vow there was neither any confusion nor any uncertainty in Rama's accepting that as an order without any risk of harm that may be done to the subjects or other people. There was no wastage of human caliber or finances as, Bharat and Shatrughna managed the things well at Ayodhaya and fought the battles with minimum resources.

Then, Organizing as a process involves[61]:

Identification of activities, Classification of grouping of activities, Assignment of duties, Delegation of authority and creation of responsibility, Coordinating authority and responsibility relationships.

Rama in exile identified the areas having shortfalls. Both brothers maintained cordial relations with the regional beings and gained various skills. These skills and relationships helped them a lot, when Sita was abducted by Ravana. Organization on a systematic note started when they had to manage with minimum resources and had to build cordial interpersonal relationships with the ruling or prominent authorities of the area, for example- both of them helped Sugriva against injustice done to him by Bali. "Managerial function of staffing involves manning the organizational structure through proper and effective selection; appraisal

& development of personnel to fill the roles designed under the structure". Staffing involves[62]:

Manpower Planning (estimating man power in terms of searching, choose the person and giving the right place), Recruitment, selection & placement.

During conversation about staffing (human resource) it is clearly observed that for performing various tasks Rama took the help of all irrespective of their age, social background, class, colour or creed, and evaluated a person on the basis of his caliber and technical skills. Distribution of work in accordance with the expertise of the person led to the successful commencement of various assignments like sending Hanuman for searching Sita, asking Nal & Neel to construct the bridge.

Direction has following elements[63]: Supervision, Motivation, Leadership, Communication

When it comes to motivate the people for getting maximum output Ramayana comes up with the best examples like Jamvant motivated Hanuman, reminded him of his latent powers, Laxmana criticized Rama for becoming very liberal to Samudra (sea) and inspired him to take some action in order to fulfil the task at hand.

"Controlling is the measurement & correction of performance activities of subordinates in order to make sure that the enterprise objectives and plans desired to obtain them as being accomplished." Therefore controlling[64] has following steps:

Establishment of standard performance, Measurement of actual performance, Comparison of actual performance with the standards and finding out deviation if any, & Corrective action

As discussed earlier, leadership is all about resolving paradoxes and crises, in the absence of clear knowledge, as where to draw the line. Great leaders try to anticipating future trends, they encourage group members not to use the best practices of others as benchmarks but to find innovative solutions so that others will use their practices as their own benchmarks. The best leaders exhibit both their values and their ethics in their leadership style and actions. In leadership ethics and values should be visible. As a leader, one should choose the values and the ethics that are most important, (the values and ethics one believes), in defining an individual's character. One has to live them evidently every day at work. Living values are one of the most powerful tools available to help one lead and influence others. Ethical leadership is given best in Ramayana,

Rama a static and dynamic leader; accepted exile without any objection, with the concept that the state can never be wrong[65]. Act according to the situation is the special feature of the epic characters. Laxmana appears as a fully dynamic character having firm faith in the karma philosophy and discarded the theory of destiny,

"Kaadar man kahun ek adhara, daiv daiv aalasi pukara"[66] (Sundarkanda)

Consult subordinates on important matters and allow them to give their opinions freely. When Vibhishan was banished, Rama took him under his protection. He then discussed it over with the various army chiefs some of whom disagreed with him. Instead of punishing them, Rama assuaged their suspicions and got them to accept his decision. Everybody felt that their opinions had been heard and that their objections had been clarified. Empowerment of subordinates to question his decisions was a key and unique quality of Rama which one cannot but help comparing with Ravana who never allowed anybody to contradict him. Empowerment of subordinates is beneficial in every sphere of management.

Code of ethics:

Rama observed ethical decision making in all spheres of his life. There are many leaders who make a sacrifice once in order to build credibility and then benefit out of it by making unethical decisions, relying on the knowledge that their initial sacrifice would make them immune to attacks[67]. Rama did not do so. Thus, when Ravana swaggered to battle on the first day without adequate preparations and was rendered weapon less by Rama, he was allowed to return to his citadel because the rules of chivalry were followed by Rama, stipulated that an unarmed enemy not be attacked. The message is, build credibility by living according to cherished values. On an ethical strategic note Rama sent Hanuman and Angad to give an opportunity to the enemy to ponder over the fight, and then to frighten them that if this is the calibre of one or two soldiers what will be, of all of them. Message is, give one chance to your enemy and if you can't escape fight with full valour.

In lack of finances and man power, to take the assistance of on hand means up to their best was the ethical strategy adopted by Rama, i.e. taking decision to fight with the help of 'vanar sena' and making Vibhishan an alley. It could be questioned that taking help of the brother of Ravana against him is not a moral indication, but the answer to it is that he never decoy Vibhishan by any means, it was he who came to Rama seeking help. He facilitates him out and had taken advantage for his own wellbeing. In no comportment it could be said that he was unreasonable in carrying the objectives.

Lord Rama was always having everything under his supervision; he used to take the feedback on regular intervals and the information about latest developments. Jamvant and Sugriv motivated Hanuman and the army of vanars respectively that though demons are having some superpowers, they are fighting for an unjust cause, on the other hand those who are fighting for Rama are standing for an ethical cause, so they should not feel scared and should hold trust in their skills and calibre which is must for winning the battle.

Then nowhere in whole Ramayana there appears lack of communication. Freedom of expression is a part and parcel of the epic. Leaders had constant communication with subordinates and kept into consideration their perspective before making the final judgement. Here we can quote the example of suggestions given by Jamvant, Sugriv and

Vibhishan to Rama. The epic also depicts proper distribution according to the levels of managers like Rama & Laxman followed by Sugriv, Jamvant & Hanuman leading the vanar soldiers.

The speciality of the epic is that with some exceptions, negative characters are also shown with some positive note,

Ravana the rival character of the epic was a well versed and skilled Brahmin; his subjects were satisfied with him. He pleased Shiva by the wondrous amount of devotion. He was an undefeatable warrior, the question comes then why Ravana is considered as a demon? It is only that in due course of time he became over ambitious, arrogant and inclined towards lust. Ravana having control over the three worlds had no reasons to fight with Rama but for maintaining his reputation he fought with him. His army was too big in comparison to Rama's; all demons were skilled and had terrible powers with them. In spite of all this Ravana was not able to defeat Rama. At one stage Ravana started taking the things for granted and used to insult people for various reasons. He stopped paying attention to the administration and followed the verdict of irresponsible people,

"Sachiv, vaiudya, guru teen jo priya bolahin ....[68]"

The ethical concept is that in spite of his knowledge about his defeat, he set an example by fighting and blessing Rama for his victory and not only this he had forgotten enmity towards them when his end was near, and lectured his traits and skills to Laxmana. It gives out that criticism and internal evaluation and proper feedback is always to be kept in consideration for the successful commencement of the system.

Ethical Plot:

Philosophers viewed ethics as a system of moral principles and the method for applying them. It deals with values relating to human conduct with respect to right and wrong of certain actions and to the goodness and badness of the motives and ends of such actions. It could be said that it is well managed, a beautiful start with the birth and marriage of Rama creating hope among people that they will get rid of the atrocities of the Ravana and so called demons. Then the exile of Lord Rama and the abduction of Sita provided an ethical ground for the battle. The ill treatment of Vibhishan by Ravana and his departure from Lanka to the shelter of Rama forms a base for the help that Rama has taken in the assassination of Ravana. Plot of the epic gives a clear glimpse of a well packed plan, its organization within a tenure of 14 years with the proper direction and having limited resources and the completion of task i.e. the end of cruelty of Ravana shows a well-managed ethical storyline in which every episode is complimenting the successful commencement of the final task, with a message that ethical management results in positive outcome[69].

Some of the tips that Ramayana gives:

Appoint right person for the job, according to skills and competence. Never permit anybody to come that much close that you may reveal your secrets. One should know how to turn enemies to his side. To always have trust in self and in own people so that with one's confidence the enemy gets half shattered. Not to lose confidence at any cost and to always carry an optimistic approach. Have bold and courageous members in team who are capable enough to startle the enemy. Give chance to enemy to surrender first unless there is no other way then to come up with war. And last how much good or strong you are never underestimate anybody.

This field is not to be confined with limited discussion but leaves many dimensions to work further.

Survival is the name of any business game. If a company wants to survive it has to think about its proceeds. The term profit in business is appropriate but 'only profit' is not acceptable at in the present anymore. It is a general notion that business and ethics are incompatible and it is not easy to establish a relationship between them. But in today's world the demand of ethical practices is increasing day by day. When Talcott Parson[70] proposed an integration view he must had an idea that coming age will be an age of integration and interdependency. Ethical behavior and business profits are combined in a new area called as "Business Ethics". Business being economic entity has a right to make profits, but at the same time it should also come up with some social responsibilities or social service. As human being is a part of society and so is the business, and then ethics forms the base of prosperous life, there comes automatically the concept of social obligation.

"Moral intelligence directs our other forms of intelligence to do something worthwhile. Moral intelligence gives the life, a purpose. Without moral intelligence, one would be able to do things and experience events, but they would lack meaning.[71]"

Ancient Hindu Philosophy gives us a view point that wealth, happiness, virtue and liberation are the essential elements of a successful life. Wealth satisfies material needs, happiness emotional needs, virtue rational, social and moral needs and liberation the final outcome. In this system happiness is higher than wealth, and virtue is higher than happiness. As liberation is the end of life we have to consider the virtues which form the base of ethics. This makes it clear that since ages the value of ethics was there for a prosperous life.

Business ethics is applied ethics. It is the application of our understanding of what is good and right to the assortment of institutions, technologies, transactions, activities and pursuits that we call business. The most influential institutions within contemporary society may be the economic institutions. The study and examination of moral and social responsibility in relation to business practice and decision making in business is known as "Business Ethics". These are designed to achieve two ends:

a. Production of the goods and services according to the various members of society (their needs and wants).

b. Distribution of these goods and services to the society as per the requirements.

Ethics can thus be defined as 'the character of a person expressed as right or wrong conduct of action'. It deals with values relating to human conduct with respect to the right and wrong of certain actions and to the goodness and badness of the motives and end of such actions. Social thinkers consider emerging ethical beliefs to be 'state of Act' legal matters, i.e. what is an ethical guideline today is often translated to a law or regulation.

The concept of ethical subjectivism and ethical relativism can't be avoided if we talk about business ethics. It is very clear by these concepts that ethics vary from person to person, organization to organization, region to region and society to society according to the needs of the people, vis-à-vis changing times.

Ethics and business according to separatist theory are termed as two different fields but then the integration theory of the modern age proved this theory wrong. In the globalized concept of today's world integration is the need. According to this approach if a business wishes to go a long way or to get the future success, it has to follow certain norms and ethics as one of the essential features.

Business ethics could be categorized under various sections such as:

a. Stakeholders Ethics

b. Environmental Ethics

c. Strategic Management Ethics

d. Marketing Ethics

e. Operational Ethics

f. Purchase Ethics

g. Human Resource Ethics

h. Financial Ethics

i. Merger/ Acquisition Ethics

It's not only about the ethics of various fields but then how to implement them is also a question. For that very purpose some codes and laws are needed to give some ethical guidelines in black and white. Then the responsibility of the top management in the implementation of the codes is another aspect in the world of business ethics.

A. **Stakeholders ethics**; in stake holder theory social responsibilities of a business set up could be categorized into 6 sections i.e. it is ethical on the part of a company to fulfil their responsibilities towards various interest groups such as :-

1. Shareholders: to invest their money with prudence in order to earn maximum profit through dividends and through increase in stock value.

2. Employees; to protect the interests of the employees in terms of wages, working conditions, atmosphere, facilities, etc. as they are the biggest asset of the organization.

3. Customers: the growth of consumerism has made the firms more aware of their duties towards consumers. It is ethical for a company to charge reasonable price for the commodities, to maintain standard of quality of goods and services, to look after the easy availability of goods and services as per the requirement of the customer. Then to abstain the company for unethical practices like hoarding, profiteering, or creating artificial scarcity and to deceive the customers by making false or misleading claims.

4. Creditors and Suppliers: these are responsible for providing inputs for production process in the form of raw material and other inputs. The responsibility of organization is to create a long term healthy business relationship with them, making prompt payments to creditors and suppliers, providing them with accurate, relevant and needed information.

5. Society: to preserve and enhance the wellbeing of society, of its members like involving organization to some charitable acts, not to flush industrial refuse in river etc., making provisions for hazardous risks.

6. Government: as government provides with the basic facilities required for the survival and growth of any business, the management should be law-abiding, to pay taxes and other duties with honesty and in time, neither influence government servants to obtain favour for the company, nor to try to use political influence in its favour.

B. **Environmental Ethics**; the organizations has to weigh environmental responsibilities against the responsibilities of the stake holders and societal benefits, as any damage caused to environment has an impact on society as well as on stakeholders.

Going green is the best way to stop environmental pollution. When a company adopts an anti-pollution environment policy, it is said to be 'going green'. In response they are likely to get economic benefits from increased efficiency. Competitive advantage is there through innovation in field of environmental protection, and then consumers, investors and employees respond positively to companies with a reputation for good environmental performance. Green initiatives in business range from environmental friendly technological innovation, green tourism, green community environmental campaigning and environmental counselling.

C. **Ethical issues in Strategic Management**; the term strategy is used in a business to describe how an organization is going to achieve its objectives and mission. Now ethical issue is that whether the company is ethical in framing the strategy? Is it keeping into consideration the stakeholders interests with their profits? Development of company's vision statement reflects its culture and values. Organization should involve the CEO's and senior managers in the development of vision statement.

Then due to the involvement of leader in long term strategic decisions, they are forced to encounter risky situations and organizations tend to reward them with huge remuneration. Leader has to maintain a healthy relationship with stake holders through knowledge contract, efficiency contract and psychological contract. Then organizations form 'remuneration committee' that determine on behalf of shareholders, the company's policies on specific remuneration package for Executive Directors and CEO's.

For the implementation of strategic change one has to be very cautious as the change could be positive and negative as well. So strategy change has to be incorporated with lot of prudence and by keeping in view the perspective of all interest groups.

Ethics has to be followed in mergers and acquisitions too as it results in exchange offers, share repurchases, going private and leveraged buyouts. During this, corporate raiders (who create an environment of threat to the stakeholders) need to be checked. This is a sensitive issue and has to be dealt with utmost care and caution as it could result in strategies like poison pills resulting in an adverse impact on stake holders. Before entering to the global strategy a company has to make a firm grip over the base area. The policies could vary as per the needs of regions but then ethics should be followed on the same parameters.

If the organization going for some basal change first it should evaluate the decision, then to judge it according to the benefit policy. Then with the help of top and middle level management there should be an establishment of moral intention and the concerned person should be directed to follow those ethical lines (corporate codes) in favour of the organization.

The relationship between employer and employee is based on a psychological contract in which both the parties are working to give favour to the other one; this has to be kept in mind while framing strategies for the workplace. Though one has to see the businesses in terms of cultural relativism but then the trust of stakeholders has to be maintained by going with the ethical concepts.

D. **Ethical issues in Marketing Management**; marketing is the interface between different and often competing value systems, the firms, the customers and other people with whom the business is associated. Marketing helps in promoting the organization as a whole.

As the product is meant for satisfying the need of customer the company needs to go ethical in its quality, what is assured is supplied to the customers. The ethical issue is when the companies which are dealing in the product injurious to public health are that they should not advertise their products and should discourage the adolescents from using it. This may appear as a setback for their organization but then this is an ethical practice giving them favour in the long run.

Another issue is related to the updating of consumer products with exorbitant prices which is again unethical as it is not giving the same product consumer requires and then the basic quality is also not retained.

Now the role of ethics in marketing is that if there is more demand of a product in the market company should not go for price rise policy to encash more benefits for own self.

They should not fluctuate the price system to make a burden on the customers. The product should be priced as per the cost. The companies should not go for promoting a brand for monetary benefits without any goodwill.

Unethical practices are carried out at places where the marketer stops distribution because of no profits. For the promotion of their goods the companies have to follow some advertising code of ethics. In a nut shell it could be said that marketer's professional conduct should follow the basic rule; not knowingly to do harm any being, the adherence to all applicable laws and regulations; accurate representation of marketer's education, training and experience; and active support, practice. In promotion of this code of ethics marketers should be honest in serving the customers, clients, employees, suppliers, distributors and the public. The company should discard any marketing which directly/indirectly making negative influence on females and children. On ethical grounds marketer should provide right information of the product to give the customers right to choose. Right to anonymity and confidentiality, right to privacy and right to safety also need to be kept in to consideration for going ethical in market.

E. **Ethical issues in Operational Management**; the most efficient/important task of an operations manager is to make efficient use of materials, capacity and knowledge available to achieve an output of the desired quality and quantity. Operation managers have to manage the management of human technology and system resources.

The role of operations manager could be classified into two sectors

1. Production sector

2. Service sector

Any mistake at the production and service level will be affecting the quality of the product and will result in loss of trust and diluted loyalty of the customers. Indirectly the ethics at this level is important for business to grow; there is less scope of any loophole if the company follows ethical norms.

Pagas and Verdin (1998) have proposed guidelines to tackle social and ethical problems in operations management. These could help in evaluating the system by examining the values of manager and of the company.

- Is the problem really what it appears to be?

- Could the action be considered legal?

- Does the management understand the position of those who oppose the action management is considering?

- The action will be giving benefit to whom and harm to whom?

- Has the operation section sought the opinion of others who are more knowledgeable on the subject and who would be objective too?

- Would the action be embarrassing if it were made known to your family, workers, friends and superiors?

Everyday decision making in operations research provides ethical dilemmas. Organizations often faced with problems relating to employees indulging in unethical practices like claiming extra allowances against poor input material performance.

F. **Ethical issues in Purchase Management**; the purchase manager plays a major role in getting the right quality of material in the right quantity at the right time. The Japanese developed the concept of JIT i.e. just in time purchasing with the objective that nothing will be produced until it is needed. The basic feature of this policy: high quality components during need, frequent shipments of small lots, a reliable transport, closer buyer-seller relationship, commitment to zero defects, stable production schedule. Companies usually adopt standard codes of ethics in purchasing. There are some unethical practices like accepting free gifts, deceiving suppliers, showing favouritism to some suppliers, revealing confidential information. These practices are not good for the personal image of purchase management and results in the deterioration of company's image on the whole.

Ethics training can help make new, inexperienced, and even seasoned buyers more aware of the consequences of unethical practices. Purchase managers by adopting ethical practice not only do a favour to their company but will be making a safe and secure position for themselves in the organization. The atmosphere of trust and responsibility prevails then, unethical practice may get short term profit for the company but the profit with name and the credibility in the market could be earned through ethics follow up.

G. **Ethical issues in Human Resource Management**; ethical organization comes from the principle of ethical selection. It is about acting in a way i.e. honest, fair, non-coercive, and legal. An ethical personnel officer evaluates the candidates for a given post on the same criterion. The first step towards ethical selection is to prevent discrimination. The relevant criteria would be the functional qualities or abilities that are required to do a job. Judging a person's qualities on the basis of age, gender, religion, nationality or social background is considered discriminatory. Then HRM ethics state that the company should not deny employment on non-referrals, over qualified grounds. Age, credentials and testing, though they are adopted as a criterion for employment but sometimes it is unethical to rely or depend only over these issues.

The system is unethical if it is depriving one who is in need or may be who could make a good benefit to the organization. Then the next criteria of ethical atmosphere i.e. equal opportunity to all the employees. Personal influence or proximity is unethical. Any hiring that is designed to function on the basis of quotas or reservations, aimed at providing opportunities for candidates from backward communities is considered a case of 'reverse discrimination'. Even though such practices are aimed at providing social justice, it is unable to accomplish the business objective of maximizing long term owner value. Though all type of reservations are unethical from its very inception. Yet even the government is not only practicing it but also promoting it for future, to help reduce inequalities and general welfare.

The next ethical issue in HRM is of remuneration, the company working on ethical note itself offers equal pay for equal work. If the organization bargains with the employees and have difference of salary as a policy then it is unethical. Contrary to it ethical remuneration never considers the need of a person, his effort to do some work and his ability as well it depends on either the set policy of organization or the results that a person is giving to the firm. Ethical remuneration recommends rewards for seniority and loyalty only when they result in contributions to long term credibility.

A business should reward the employees who have willingly forgone their pay rise when the business faced a financial crunch. It is unethical for the business to dishonour its commitments to employees once business is back to normal. When organization fails to honour its commitments, the employee's trust is broken and this leads to decreased long term owner value.

The turn of new millennium saw the world economies slump. Many industries were compelled to retrench or lay off people. Firing to be ethical should be honest, fair, legal and without coercion or physical violence. Firing is a critical decision which affects the reputation of the business. It creates an atmosphere of fear and uncertainty. It is unethical as it depletes the trust which is essential for business to survive and make profits.

H. **Ethical issues in Finance**; all business dealings invaridly involve finance. When businesses are weakened due to bad debts or mismatched funding or under capitalization, companies are often tempted to falsify the accounts. The importance of ethics in financial management comes in. Companies usually maintain two sets of accounts; financial those are given to the shareholders and the internal management one. Misinterpreting financial information has a negative impact on the long term owner value. Few steps should be taken into consideration for true, fair and reliable management, like ; determining the key elements of the business like the objectives of the firm and see how they are defined and measured, making sure that the funds are allocated to different activities on the basis of their importance.

Then framing of rules have a positive effect on business activities. It is important to ensure that each project or department is allotted its fair share and that the projected earnings of the department are in accordance with the funds allocated.

I. **Mergers & Acquisitions;** Ethical management has to take care during mergers and acquisitions, the financial interest of stakeholders and shareholders of the organization. Takeovers generally involve breach of trust as they transfer wealth to the shareholders by isolating implicit contracts with other stakeholders. It implies that a supplier or the employees who expect security for their work can be ignored during takeovers. The ethics say that each group involved must agree to respect certain contracts or promises, for example if a firm promises performance based bonus for employees and the company that acquires does not take this policy into account then it would be unethical and employees would feel demotivated and would not perform as per the expectations which may result in poor work performance.

The hostile takeovers disagreement over the prices and some popular ways like poison pills, greenmail, golden parachute, people pill, sandbag etc. when are practiced results in unethical management. Management buyouts and money laundering are also unethical in mergers and acquisitions. So the ethical management makes the companies not to follow these practices in favour of the firm.

The firms generally face ethical issues in financing too. In general businesses practice some types of frauds to make more money like-

1. Fictitious revenues which are shown in the books but are not actually earned.

2. Another way companies overstate assets and income is, by taking advantage of the accounting cut off period either to boost sales or reduce liabilities and expenses (fraudulent timing differences.)

3. Concealed liabilities and expenses that are not shown in the financial statements of a company.

4. Improper fraudulent disclosure or omissions that results in materially misleading financial statements.

5. Fraudulent asset valuation that takes place usually in estimating the inventory.

To cope up with manipulations in financial statements, it is important to know the types of accounts of an organization. These are of 2 types –

a) Financial account; Reported to the shareholders, a report that is submitted to the public. So this reporting need to be ethical as trust and confidence of shareholders to the company is the biggest asset.

b) Internal management account; these show internal operations of the business and its financial activities. This helps the management to maintain a trustworthy internal account, essential for a business to function smoothly.

Transparency in financial matters gives a clean image to the organization in auditing and a positive response from the society and employees as well.

Ethics is a complex subject and its history is filled with diverse theories that are systematically refuted by rival theories. These are some of the issues related to role of ethics in business, which complements a view that has become increasingly accepted during the last few years – which ethical behaviour is the best long term business strategy for a company.

In fine it could be said that ethics indirectly exerts a paramount of influence on all departments of our practical life. It helps to overcome ethical dilemmas, allowing for the right choice, and this not only benefits the company in making a good reputation in the society but also earn monetary benefit in the long run. As the people start relying on the organization and the company would be getting permanent and reliable stakeholders for its success. We have to be open to the world of our philosophy, "We have to keep our eyes open, find out problems and seek the inspiration of the past in solving them. The spirit of truth never clings to its forms but ever renews them." So, business system as a subsystem to the social system should promote ethics for improving health and wealth of the society consistently.

At the same time some suggestions could enhance the role of ethics in business, like: Companies should focus on long term perspective instead of the short terms. There should be training in all the organizations to train the people to follow up of ethics. Thus ethical environment should be developed and encouraged by the company in name of corporate codes. Corporate codes of ethics are often viewed cynically as attempts to foster good public relations or to reduce legal liability; it is a reasonable model for understanding how we should articulate moral principles and introduce them into business practice Periodic review should be a part of regular intervals. Ethics should flow from top level management as an example for others. Ethics should be slated as the social responsibility, and should be inculcated at the graduation level in the coming times.

End Notes:

1.   Bono Edward De, Teach Yourself To Think, Penguin Books, 1996, England, p

2. Esquivel Adolfo Perez, Opening the Doors of Hope in the New Millennium, Harmony & Peace, Ed. T.D.Singh, Delhi Peace Summit & Bhaktivedanta Institute Kolkata, p 226

3. Hudson Tim, Think Better, Tata McGraw Hill, New Delhi, 2008, p 15

4. Joseph P T, SJ, EQ & Leadership, Tata McGraw Hill, New Delhi, 2007, p 42

5. Sen Amartya, The Argumentative Indians, Penguin Books, London, 2005, p 345

6. Roger Martin & Hilary Austin, The Art of Integrative Thinking, source Internet.

7. Ibid

8. Carnegie Dale, How to stop worrying and Start Living, Pocket Books, New York, 1984, p 46

9. Ibid, p 208

10. Basham A.L. Edi., A Cultural History of India, (J Duncan M. Derrett,Social and Political Thoughts and Institutions), Oxford University Press, N.Delhi, 2006, p124

11. Ibid 3, p 228

12. Haines Stephen G, Successful Strategic Planning, Crisp Publications, USA, 1995, p 7

13. Sasson Remez, Mind Power and Success, Success Consciousness. com

14. Ibid 3, p 218

15. Covey Stephen R, The 7 Habits of Highly Effective People, Pocket Books, London, 2004, p 288

16. Martin Roger L, The Opposable Mind Winning Through Integrative Thinking, USA, 2009, p 22

17. Ibid, p 6

18. Chakraborty S K & Chakraborty Debangshu, Culture Society & Leadership – Spiritual Perspectives,The ICFAI University Press, Hyderabad,2006, p-65

19. Source Internet

20. Ibid 1, p 32, 47

21. Roy Arundhati, The God of Small Things, Penguin Books, New Delhi,2002, p 331-2

22. Ibid 4, p 345

23. Ibid 15, p 318

24. Ibid 6

25. Eliot T.S., Little Gidding (the last of his Four Quartets),1942, British (US-born) critic, dramatist & poet (1888 - 1965)

26. Weihrich Heinz & Koontz Harold, Management A Global Perspective, 10th ed., Tata Mc Graw Hill, New Delhi, 2001, p-490

27. North house Peter G, Leadership, SAGE Pub. India Pvt. Ltd., New Delhi, 2007, p-9

28. Weihrich Heinz & Koontz Harold, Management A Global Perspective, 10th ed., Tata Mc Graw Hill, New Delhi, 2001, p-9

29. Ibid, p-9

30. Giri Bhuwan, Managerial Leadership, V l, Mittal Pub., New Delhi, 2009, p-39

31. Joseph P T, SJ, EQ and Leadership, Tata McGraw Hill, New Delhi, 2007, p- 18

32. Chakraborty S K & Chakraborty Debangshu,Rajarshi: The Quintessential Indian Model of Leadership, Culture Society & Leadership – Spiritual Perspectives, The ICFAI University Press, Hyderabad,2006, p- 77

33. Collins Jim, Good to Great, Harper Collins Publishers Inc., New York, 2001, p -28

34. Ibid, p – 57

35. Ibid, p – 142

36. James Macgregor Burns, Leadership, Harper & Row, 1978

37. Cohen William A, The New Art of the Leader, Viva Books, New Delhi, 2003, p-1

38. Ibid, p -277

39. Sen Amartya, The Argumentative Indians, Penguin Books, London, 2005, p- 339

40. Giri Bhuwan, Managerial Leadership, Cohen William A Vol. I, Mittal Pub., New Delhi, 2009, p – 68

41. North house Peter G, Leadership, SAGE Pub. India Pvt. Ltd., New Delhi, 2007, p- 11

42. Woolfe Lorin, The Bible on Leadership, Jaico Pub. House, Mumbai, 2008, p-113, 115

43. Arise Awake an Exhibition on Swami Vivekananda, Sri Ramkrishna Ashram, Mysore, 2002, panel 40

44. Arise Awake an Exhibition on Swami Vivekananda, Sri Ramkrishna Ashram, Mysore, 2002, panel 27

45. Tichy Noel, The Leadership Engine, Harper Business, New York, 1997

46. Tagore Rabindranath, Omnibus III, Rupa & Co., New Delhi, 2005, p -8

47. Business Ethics & Corporate Governance, Fed Uni (Federation of Universities), 2003.

48. Joseph P T, SJ, EQ & Leadership, Tata McGraw Hill, New Delhi, 2007

49. ibid

50. http://www.action-wheel.com/ethics-in-leadership.html

51. Sinha Jadunath, A Manual of Ethics, New Central Book Agency, Kolkata, 1978.

52. http://humanresources.about.com/od/leadership/a/leader_values.htm

53. Sen Amartya, 'The Argumentative Indians', Penguin Books, London, 2005.

54. Radhakrishnan S, 1999, Indian Philosophy, Vol.2, Oxford University Press, New Delhi.

55. Tripathi P C & Reddy P N, Principles of Management, Tata McGraw Hill, New Delhi, 2006.

56. Sen Amartya, The Argumentative Indians, Penguin Books, London, 2005

57. P.C.Tripathi & P.N.Reddy, Principles of Management, Tata McGraw-Hill Publishing Company Limited, New Delhi, 2006

58. ibid.

59. Tulsidas, Ramcharitmanas, Geeta Press Gorakhpur.

60. Covey, S.R. (1989), The Seven Habits of Highly Effective People, Free Press New York.

61. http://gbr.pepperdine.edu/2010/08/ six-components-of-a-model-for-workplace-spirituality/

62. Introduction to Management, ICFAI Center for Management Research, Hyderabad, 2004.

63. ibid.

64. P.C.Tripathi & P.N.Reddy, Principles of Management, Tata McGraw-Hill Publishing Company Limited, New Delhi, 2006

65. http://www.scribd.com/ sspillai/d/24652526-Ramayana-Mangement-Ethics

66. Tulsidas, Ramcharitmanas, Geeta Press Gorakhpur.

67. Joseph P T, SJ, EQ & Leadership, Tata McGraw Hill, New Delhi, 2007, p-42

68. Tulsidas, Ramcharitmanas, Geeta Press Gorakhpur.

69. Concepts of workplace spirituality, http://www.mbaknol.com/management-concepts/concept-of-workplace-spirituality.

70. Business Ethics & Corporate Governance, Fed Uni (Federation of Universities), 2003.

71. Joseph P T, SJ, EQ & Leadership, Tata McGraw Hill, New Delhi, 2007

Chapter 3

Variation That Ethics Can Procure

Transformation indicates a change towards positivity for the benefit of individual as well as for the well being of society. Persuasion is an art which makes the people follow their role model, and when the role model does it with truthfulness and humanitarian perspective it is spirituality. Though it has nothing to do with the formal rituals of religion but has to do a lot with the philosophical perception of the same. The one who is able to persuade the people to follow righteous path for the betterment of society is a spiritual leader. One who can inculcate the confidence to live for the virtuous path with the established philosophy of religion is the leader in true sense. Leaders of today talk a lot about justice, equality, human rights etc. but many of them are not living them. We need to know how value based spiritual leadership is the need of hour.

"Moral intelligence gives the life, a purpose. Without moral intelligence, one would be able to do things and experience events, but they would lack meaning. Moral intelligence directs our other forms of intelligence to do something worthwhile".

I was watching a movie "Hate story" and felt the heat of female revenge in that. Somewhere it gave a glimpse of inner beast underneath human skin. I am unable to decide the effect movie left in my mind in particular, and the public in general . Is the perception of writer is righteous? How many audiences could take the undercurrent message? Wouldn't it will be a perplexing movie for the teenagers? Some of these queries crept to my sensibility and I asked a question to myself, are we really progressing with these transformations? What if the audience will be taking the issues of both the sides? How many common herds will be able to catch the heat of the issue?

What is the significance of the mention of this here? The answer is, that masses pursue whatever is projected in entertainment agency, it acts as a leader for them, as leadership is followership[1].

'Transformation' the very basic nature of this word is, change for betterment. Since ages the preachers played a role of transformational leaders. They guide us to mark out the fine and thin boundary line between right and wrong and helped the society in virtuous decisions. Sorry to say that we are shame less creatures, who look for personal benefit in each and everything, and we use to manipulate the preaching also for material gains. The point is not to discard them but then why we are so week to look for our gains at the cost of somebody's loss? In order to make our line lengthy, we erase the one drawn by others. Why our leaders of vivid fields are not able to instigate us to follow up there preaching?

Transformation and change are two different processes and occur at different levels of reality. Transformation takes place within. It happens in our cells, in our thoughts and perceptions, in how we look at the world and who we choose to be in relationship to it. Change, happens outside. We change our plans, change our diet, and change our strategy, change partners, change personnel. And that change so often comes out of reaction to a problem or simply out of boredom with doing things the same way[2]. Transformation is a wider term, when a dacoit turns to sage Valmiki, when an offspring follows the words of parents to make them happy, when a case changes the life of a lawyer, and a teacher sets a live example of values, it is there. According to social and natural norms transformation is an optimistic term and that is why it is a key to prosperity.

A discussion over this expanse is required because today we can see the negativity creeping over the positivity in all the strata of society. Politicians, religious preachers, administrative officers, teachers, lawyers, entrepreneurs, social workers, business tycoons to common man, anybody can be a leader, but how far the basic principles of leadership are followed? Inspiration by a leader often plays a major role in spurring people on to maximum performance, not only this but the second stage of performance management is encouragement[3]. Leaders are there to reform the society in its visual inception as well as to its basic soul. Even a revolutionary leader has to have something in store for preserving the goodness of society. So it could be said that leadership can come in a range of forms like charismatic, visionary, spiritual, trait based, practical etc. but the transformation from existing stage to an enhanced one is a common feature of all of them, i.e. though transformational leadership is a separate field of leadership studies but it remains latent in each type of leadership studies.

Confidence building, money making, becoming successful in material world is the need of hour, a good social status is essential in ambitious world of today. A world which is full of crimes, corruption, unemployment, poverty, shaky relationships, cut throat competitions and dying sensitivity one has to struggle for survival. And it does not end here with this, entire internal struggle between mind and heart of an individual is there too.

We need a support to sail smoothly through this journey of life, with such a social set up and ambitions, and that is what we call as transformational leadership. For finding a solution to any problem leaders work with three tools of-brainstorming, psychological techniques, and analysis of alternatives[4]. It is something which can make us meets our own soul; listen to the voice coming from within, which we crush often. Life is a journey and that too with lots of ups and down, at times we come across the situations when the world wide philosophy is unable to respond, there we need transformational leadership.

Kautilya to Ambedkar, Eienstien to Charles Babbage, Kalidas to Shakespeare, Bill Gates to Ratan Tata, Tagore to Premchand, Prithviraj Kapoor to Mahesh Bhatt, classes to masses everybody is having a unique style of reformation, but the problem is of misinterpretation, as what to take up and what not? This is the stage where conflicts and compromises go hand in hand, and logical analysis is required, there we need a proper guidance of transformation.

Bhagawat Gita states that, "the one who controls the senses by the trained and purified mind and intellect, and engages

the organs of action to selfless service is considered superior",
i.e. moral leadership is powerful and it can work wonders.
Leadership needs to be ethical in nature only then its true
purpose is solved. Since ages the leaders of all fields are
considered to be the perfect and sensitive people who can
fight for another's cause. It can be said that leadership and
ethics go hand in hand. One can only feel to fight for justice
when values are there. This lesson of life starts at an early
stage of upbringing and the outcome is welfare of the society.
This important instrument of leadership stands throughout
history as a fundamental aspect of living.

Leadership values can be classified as; Ethical virtues: old
fashioned character tests such as sobriety, chastity, abstention,
kindness, altruism and other; "Ten commandments" rules of
personal conduct such as honesty, integrity, trustworthiness,
reliability, reciprocity, accountability; Moral values such
as order or security, liberty, equality, justice, community
(meaning brother hood and sisterhood).

Transforming leaders are idealized in the sense that they
are a moral exemplar of working towards the benefit of the
team, organization and/or community.

Charismatic, Engaging, Inspirational, Stable, Optimistic,
Encouraging, Honest, Motivational, Respectful, Positive,
Team oriented, Effective communicator, Empowering,
Reliable, Trustworthy, Empathetic, Mentor, Visionary etc.
are considered the traits[5] of transformational leadership.
These traits are sensed spiritual too in nature. These leaders
can create a win-win scenario in which the employees enjoy
working for the organization which results in manifold

increase in prosperity. Quality of life improves since it is independent of material success[6]. It is a great asset as it opens up the possibility of merging the spiritual pursuit and professional pursuit. Not only for the followers but for the one who is leading it gives much.

Once you solve the problems of man to your own satisfaction, you had your philosophy of life and evolved your own art of living, all this you must apply to the present situation and out of it will arise a new creation and not a mere repetition, a creation which the soul of your people will own for itself and proudly offer to the world as its tribute to the welfare of man[7].

Family members, teachers and elderly people can play this role of mentor and can act as the transformational leader, but for that very purpose they need to set themselves as an example. The logic and reasoning which is applicable at the family level could further be extended to the national and international perspective too.

The need of hour is to make people courageous from within; intellectual stimulation for innovative precepts, to come up with their creativity in favour of society, to manage the situations has to be taught. Inspirational motivation is the third element about optimism, vision, building confidence, etc. Today it is a difficult job to find such leadership in tough world of competition and favouritism. Idealized influence is the last element of transformational leadership. To be there as a role model, for respect and trust, indirect instilling the ethics to the surrounding solves the purpose.

This is the high time, there is a need to ponder over the words of American writer James Allen, "You are today where your thoughts have brought you, and you will be tomorrow where your thoughts take you, you cannot escape the result of your thoughts"[8]. Now a day there is a worldwide discussion on visionary abilities, on character, on heroism, in leadership roles. All the Rajarshi type leaders in India's history had been constructively charismatic, visionary heroic, and were free from the bane of narcissism. Why? Because, they were close to truth as joy. Studies of their lives reveal two mutually consistent, abiding endeavors; - Self-control and renunciation[9].

Many organizations need more than minor "tweaking". They need to be transformed from one thing to another. This requires a talented leader who possesses certain traits and skills. Transformational leadership is a theory that was developed by James McGregor Burns in 1978. He developed this theory to further address the aspects of an organization that lead to success, encourage enthusiasm among an organization's employees, and identify the values employees place on their work[10]. True leaders enjoy the trust of others, which is very different from enjoying the perks and flattery and power that ego insists are the signs of being a leader. Trust has to be given in order to receive trust[11] which is the very base of transformation. In order to get into the essence of transformation, leader has to be always ready with his soul and heart for followers. True leaders offer trust, encouragement, and congratulations as others find their own way[12].

This concern is not to be viewed as a mere academic product but as an expression of many sided activities. A person may have all the traits of a leader, but if he/she doesn't personally see to the development of new leaders the organization won't be sustainable[13]. As a development tool, transformational leadership has spread already in all sectors of western societies, including governmental organizations. Various think tanks are coming up with the spread of this perception, where nurturing of innovative ideas is the prime focus.

In this material race of globalization some change is required from within, which can rectify the system, give spiritual vision to the masses and serenity to the society. It is assumed that leaders never want to become larger than life heroes. They never aspire to be put on a pedestal or become unreachable icons. They are seemingly ordinary people quietly producing extraordinary results[14]. It is seen that only 'change' is constant in this world, and that has to be carried on by leaders for welfare state. It is a fact that leadership has an extraordinary power, but it has been advised to leaders that they may not treat princes as princes but they should treat persons as persons[15], so that the concept of egalitarian society with individual prosperity is meeting out.

Transformation is not a new concept, but it needs be re-established, as in, rat race we confine ourselves to our vested interests and forget the philosophy of 'Vasudhaiv Kutumbakam'. Leaders of all arenas have to analyze the fact that positivity from within is accountable for miracles over ages, so that has to be there with soul, it should be nurtured with utmost care and perseverance for a welfare state and prosper individuals.

The secret of life lies in honesty and bravery, numbers do not count, nor does wealth or poverty, a handful of men can throw the world off its hinges, provided they are united in thought, word and deed[16]. The relevance of these details can be observed in life time to time when we say, teach yourselves, teach everyone his real nature, call upon the sleeping soul and see how it awakes. Power will come, glory will come, goodness will come, purity will come and everything that is excellent will come when the sleeping soul is roused to self-conscious activity[17].

In fine it could be said, "Transformational leadership gives an opportunity to explore the world logically and rationally, from different dimensions which favour the philosophy of prosperity for ages and for generations, as",

"We shall not cease from exploration

And the end of all our exploring

Will be to arrive where we started

And know the place for the first time."[18]

'Work is worship', is an illustrious proverb. When working came into inception the very first philosophy treated it as something to be done religiously. The piousness and allegiance were the traits, why these 'were' the traits? Because in due course of time the sanctity of mind and spirit towards work was dissolved and materialism weighed heavier. The belonging of workplace is not the pace of the day rather it is, how to keep oneself detached with organization focusing only on making money. Spirituality is inside integrity of a person which works for the wellbeing of all without causing any harm to anybody and then to work for the upliftment of all at personal and professional level.

We have to ponder that what are the reasons behind this change in approach? Is it good for organization and employee or not? If it is harmful then what are the area in which it has to be curtailed? In spite of number of spiritual Gurus and reforming centers why the animal instincts of human beings are still increasing multi dimensionally.

The chirping of birds in the morning is a scene rare to be found in concrete metropolitans, and not only there but in villages too. Urbanization stole from us the natural beauty and on the same footage materialism has stolen the piousness of inner self.

In this rat race there are many challenges that society is facing in political, social, economic, administrative, ethical arenas. A slight ponder makes it clear that the root confront is the challenge of self-bankrupt i.e. people have no control over their emotions rather they don't wish to have any rule book for their own self.

Everything appears to be a matter of profit only, be it in form of some material or other benefit. Such hue and cry these days over various social issues is the result of lack of spirituality at workplace. There was a time when work was considered as worship and it was done religiously with full honesty, but today in majority it is done for the sake of doing it. Observance from a minor to a major level gives the same result. From a labour to the key position holders all are busy in making their job that too by hook or crook. People know that if they won't be compromising with their boss they may lose the job as the queue outside the office is quiet long. The one whose job is secure takes it as an advantage that he needs not to worry about job security whether he puts up the labour required for the job or not, so he gives up working and enjoy the privileges given. It could be said that one reason behind this casual approach is the constraints of private job and benefits of public one.

Secondly there is stress that penetrated to our nerves in last two decades; it is the stress to earn more, to prove oneself, to have financial and social status, to be at the top, to maintain shattered relationships. In order to fulfil these we compromised with our work and deliberately stopped piousness to it, as many other tasks appear to be of much importance.

This approach gives rise to a self-centric personality, and selfishness can never be spiritual. Our motto should be that what we have taken from world, culture and society we have to return that back, but the fact is that this sensitivity is missing.

A teacher is interested only in completion of course, doctor diagnose two additional diseases with the actual one, advocates brawl for the party which could pay better, files are kept on pending for years in govt. departments. Religious and spiritual leaders, only sermonize instead of putting up live example of their own, media is busy in sensation, and political leaders to lure the voters, students are busy with brands and models and parents in giving them money in place of time.

In fine it could be said that from politicians to administrators, judiciary to social workers, business men to service class, literary laureates to scientists, classes to masses,: the direct or indirect work is done only for the sake of work, not perceived with the intention of organizational welfare resulting in development of society. In this scenario it is funny to expect from people to think workplace religiously theirs'. Spirituality is so much in air these days but not to follow rather to use it as a status symbol (refined religious approach of vision.)

By this time a natural question is likely to come to the mind of readers why such an importance is given to the word 'spirituality' at workplace. The reason is that spirituality affects an organizational performance positively. It is expected to moderate the relationship between negative perceptions of the organization and organizational cynicism. In organizations which try to improve the spiritual development of their members, creativity increase, team performance satisfaction and organizational commitment have been reported[19] very high. It is believed that encouraging spirituality in the workplace would be advantageous for the organization. Popularity of spirituality in workplace is a tool that guarantees the survival of the organizations against current uncertain environment. Not only has this but it also guaranteed personal up gradation of an individual in person as well as in professional mode. If the individual is having a strong sense of spirituality, cynicism may be reduced, as the person feels an internal sense of purpose surrounding his/her life, and believes that there is higher meaning for the events that occur in all the aspects of life[20].

Now the burning issue is that if it is of that much importance why it is complicated to practice it? There might be many reasons like personal stress, to accomplish certain targets and goals. In order to maintain social and financial status, to backstab to take erroneous measures come out to be a short way to success. Then with privatization and some technical loopholes in administration insecurity among people is observed. This fear of survival stops them to be ethical as it comes to their job. Then again as a fault of system many non-deserving people enjoy the benefits given by govt. And the deserving ones left out with no option to make their ends meet by hook or crook. Last but not the least reason is that today, the classes provide the mechanic and calculative lessons to earn bread instead of providing an amalgamation in proper ratio of both ethics and knowledge.

These rationale emerge as a threat to the credibility of any organization, as a result of the mentioned reasons, there appears lack of enthusiasm among employees, nonperformance, enhancement of materialism approach, increase in inside organization corruption, increase in personal weaknesses of the employees which again is harmful for any organization.

Contrary to it, Spiritual perception not only improves efficiency, but more importantly reaches a relaxation and inner satisfaction along with a long happiness and provides a cordial environment among coworkers which ultimately may lead to success of organization and employee as well. A spiritual organization in addition to employees' satisfaction raise, improve honesty, confidence, respect, responsibility, and personal stability in the workplace[21]. Spirituality tends to increase the belonging of an employee to his / her workplace.

Employee morale has a direct influence on productivity, which is why organizations spend large sums of money trying to make working environments comfortable, pleasant, and even luxurious. When sincerity and pure motives are combined with highly developed business leadership and consistent decision making skills, the outcome is a powerful and highly motivated organization. In searching for business solutions, one must be innovative in developing ways to positively impact not only the client but also co-workers and peers. "Spirituality in the Workplace" is more than just a concept; it is a practical method for attaining business success[22].

One spiritual commentator describes prayers and mediation as remedies for clearing the clogged arteries of our soul. Because individual needs differ, just as our appetite for food and its consumption diverges, everybody responds in a different manner. At the end of the day, we are all human beings with hearts and souls. Everyone has different lives and different issues; however one thing that unites us – especially in the workplace—is that we are all trying to do our best and to have our work appreciated, for the benefit of making the world a better place to live. Contentment in the workplace, bred by a sense of spiritual fulfilment, is in every bit a valuable commodity. Our attitudes and entitlement take on a different shape only when we are on the receiving end of the treatment we wish all would aspire to[23].

"The way 'spirituality' is often used suggests that we exist solely as a collection of individuals, not as members of a religious community, and that religious life is merely a private journey."[24] Although religion affects individual's spirituality and plays an important role in governing our day to day behaviour at work through ritual practices but the religion should not be interpreted in terms of spirituality, because spirituality is personal; religion is social[25].

Characteristics of a Spiritual Workplace: Suggestions as Well

Regardless of this ongoing debate, identifying desired characteristics of spiritual workplaces can bring us closer to understanding the role that spirituality can play in organizations, the way it can function to positively impact the bottom line, and the value it might bring to members of the work community.

Spirituality may be thought as an incompatible with modern trends of the day, but still deep somewhere it can provide insight to the mankind and organizations. The mentioned six effects[26] can be associated with a model of workplace spirituality. It Emphasizes Sustainability, Values Contribution, Prizes Creativity, Cultivates Inclusion, Develops Principles, Promotes Vocation.

A systemic view of work and contribution in the world promotes links between sustainability and an awareness of limited resources. This approach to design, production, and commerce is being increasingly associated with spirituality because it seeks to contribute to the greater good in the world. An understanding of sustainable growth and development includes a well-thought-out strategy that identifies potential long-term impacts or implications of actions. Not only in one field or the other but wherever pious goals are there sustainability comes.

More than providing excellent service for customers, global service indicates a larger sense of responsibility to contribute to the betterment of the world. While the local family business may not provide products and services that will improve the quality of life in third world countries, some companies historically have fundamentally understood that they have to make the world a better place through the products or services that they sell. Today's spiritual organization is deliberate in implementing a vision that is built around contributions to the betterment of mankind. It promotes work outside of the organization that contributes to and "gives back" to society through community and volunteer service. Spiritually aware managers and businesses consider themselves servants of employees, customers, and the community.

Creativity is a necessary part of the development cycle; it is the key to successfully navigating changes. The artistic industries have long ago recognized the spiritual nature of individual and group creative processes, and many educators understand the importance of seamless, daily incorporation of creativity in helping their students learn. A spiritual workplace provides resources to help people to uncover their creative potential and to practice creativity within the organization.

The spiritual organization respects and values individuals' life experiences and the lessons learned from them. Such an organization is intentional in its efforts to include individuals who bring appropriate skill sets to a particular job, but who may have been excluded historically from participating in a professional community of practice due to circumstances they did not choose. Such historic exclusion from the workplace has included people with physical disabilities, people whose skin colour or ethnic origin differs from those of the majority population, and those who have been discriminated against due to gender or sexual orientation. Increasingly, corporations are seeing the value of their employees working together in community toward a commonly held vision. They have a sense that the concepts of love and acceptance within a cultural context of care builds a sense of community that supports the work of the company and that has a direct impact on the bottom line.

Organizations have to realize the benefits of treating the people by actively supporting the formulation of ethical principles that promote personal growth, long-term character development, and personal connections of faith and work development. Assisting employees in integrating personal growth, learning, and faith with job performance benefits the organization. This type of principled emphasis includes providing resources that help employees to understand themselves better, develop successful professional and personal relationships, and enhance personal management skills. Employees need to be encouraged to develop an accurate and realistic sense of the impact that other people have on them and the impact that they have on others.

Organizations have to be aware of the benefits of shared ownership of corporate values by every member of the organization. By acknowledging that one's general search for spiritual growth and fulfilment need not be separate from one's work, organizations lay the groundwork for spiritual development to assist in engendering understanding among employees. Companies that understand workplace spirituality go beyond being supportive of learning and development by helping employees develop a sense of "calling" or identification of passion about their lives and their work. Companies required emphasizing the discovery and appropriate utilization of individual's caliber and encouraging employees to use their unique skills within the organization. Grounded religious faith development is recognized as an important and deeply personal part of growth for many people, one that can help them more easily recognize their vocations.

The six components presented here as building blocks toward considering a model of workplace spirituality serve as a partial framework for engaging in a broader conversation of spirituality's place and influence in culture. The recent trend is to recognize the spiritual nature of people and the importance of incorporating the "whole person" at work.

Certain virtues such as courage, honesty, fairness and empathy are considered as traits necessary for ethical behaviour[27]; Emotions organize intellectual capacities and indeed create the sense of self[28]. Spirituality fosters these traits and emotions resulting in preparation of a serene and cordial atmosphere at workplace.

Spirituality in this new sense is a private activity, although it may be pursued with a group of the like-minded, it is not 'institutional' in that it does not involve membership in a group that has claims on its members.

Spirituality is the state of intimate relationship with the inner self of higher values and morality as well as recognizing the truth of inner nature of people. The concept of spirituality at work place can be explained as an experience of interconnectedness, shared by all those involved in the work process, initially triggered by the awareness that each is individually driven by an inner power, which raises and maintains his/her sense of honesty, kindness and courage, consequently leading to the collective creation of an aesthetically motivational environment characterized by a sense of purpose, high ethical standards, acceptance, peace, trust, thus establishing an atmosphere of enhanced team performance and overall harmony[29].

End notes:

1.   Weihrich Heinz & Koontz Harold, Management A Global Perspective, 10th ed., Tata Mc Graw Hill, New Delhi, 2001, p-490

2. http://www.transformationalpresence.org/articles/ transformational-leadership-blazing-new-trails-toward-a-world- that-works#,

3. Woolfe Lorin, The Bible on Leadership, Jaico Pub. House, Mumbai, 2008, p-113, 115

4. Cohen William A, The New Art of the Leader, Viva Books, New Delhi, 2003, p-277

5. http://en.wikipedia.org/wiki/Transformational_leadership)

6. ibid.

7. Tagore Rabindranath, Omnibus III, Rupa & Co., New Delhi, 2005, p -8

8. Giardina Ric, Living a Balanced Life, Infinity Books, New Delhi, 2005, p-29

9. Chakraborty S K & Chakraborty Debangshu,Rajarshi: The Quintessential Indian Model of Leadership, Culture Society & Leadership – Spiritual Perspectives, The ICFAI University Press, Hyderabad,2006, p- 77)

10. http://en.wikipedia.org/wiki/Transformational_leadership)

11. Dyer W.Wayne, Wisdom of the Ages, Thorsons, New York, 1999, p-10

12. Ibid.

13. Tichy Noel, The Leadership Engine, Harper Business, New York, 1997

14. Collins Jim, Good to Great, Harper Collins Publishers Inc., New York, 2001, p -28

15. James Macgregor Burns, Leadership, Harper & Row, 1978

16. Arise Awake an Exhibition on Swami Vivekananda, Sri Ramkrishna Ashram, Mysore, 2002, panel 40

17. Arise Awake an Exhibition on Swami Vivekananda, Sri Ramkrishna Ashram, Mysore, 2002, panel 27

18. Eliot T.S., Little Gidding (the last of his Four Quartets),1942. (British (US-born) critic, dramatist & poet (1888 - 1965)

19. Neck, C.P.and Milliman, J.F. (1994), *Thought self leadership: finding spiritual fulfilment in organizational life,* Journal of Managerial Psychology, Vol. 9, No. 8, p-9.

20. Weitz Ely, Vardi Yoav, Setter Ora, *Does Workplace Spirituality Mitigate the Intention of Employees to Engage in Organizational Misbehaviour?* An Initial Research Agenda, ISOL 2011, Vol. III, p-421.

21. Campuzano, Lydia Guadalupe;Seteroff, Sviatoslav Steve;(2009): *A new approach to a spiritual business organization and employee satisfaction,* Eastern Academy of Management.

22. http://www.businesstoday.org/magazine/ temporarily-cancelled-running-bull/spirituality-workplace

23. ibid

24. Bellah, Robert. (2004). An interview published in *Tricycle: The Buddhist Review*. August, (New York, NY: The Tricycle Foundation).

25. Kozney, G. (2004) *Dancing with Dogmas: The fine line between religion and spirituality. Communities*, 124

26. http://gbr.pepperdine.edu/2010/08/ six-components-of-a-model-for-workplace-spirituality/

27. Covey, S.R. (1989), *The Seven Habits of Highly Effective People*, Free Press New York.

28. Joseph P T, SJ, *EQ & Leadership*, Tata McGraw Hill, New Delhi, 2007, p-42

29. *Concepts of workplace spirituality*, http://www.mbaknol.com/ management-concepts/concept-of-workplace-spirituality

Chapter 4

How To Inculcate Ethics

Literature is the mirror of society, is a very well said quote. In every era the need of literature is felt. We can say that literature is the food to soul. How literature can change our perception and how it can motivate us to live a life of virtues is the burning discussion. The emotions and morality could be taught in an indirect method by the study of literature. In today's scenario when materialism is the prime focus youngsters are losing the ethics of life, if literature departments are not taken care then the aroma of nature will not be there and the society will be a place of dry concrete only.

Science and language alone cannot fulfil the need of hour; we need good human beings for a good and prosperous society. The perspectives given by the writers help the people to become sensitive, moral and courageous for prosperity in life. It is an inseparable part of life; it should be nurtured to its fullest. "Literature adds to reality, it does not simply describe it. It enriches the necessary competencies that daily life requires and provides; and in this respect, it irrigates the deserts that our lives have already become." – C.S.Lewis.

The famous minute written by Macaulay on Indian education in 1935 was dictated by an educational, indeed, a literary aim[1]. Macaulayan syllabus, claimed that only great and serious literature should be taught and not the language.

The standard canon of English literature from Chaucer and Shakespeare, Milton, Dryden, Pope, Wordsworth, Coleridge, Shelley to Browning was read in original for its elevating and enlightening functions[2].

The concrete and strong ground on which we are standing today is the gift of that era in which the knowledge is shared through fairy tales and stories. One of the great features of life today is the curious shrinkage of the world. The invention of various modes of conveyance and communication like air services and internet, have helped to annihilate space. Of their scientific importance and social value there is no need to speak here; but the cumulative effect of these things upon the psychology of the day is worth noting, in as much as it reacts upon our literature[3]. The primitive as well as the contemporary literature make us grow as balanced personality because it imparts us vision to think logically. 'Literature is the mirror of society', true, and we are developing by tracing out flaws and rectifying them through that mirror.

An individual's persona consists of perfect balance of mind and heart. Mechanic era of today only requires professional dealing everywhere without sentiments. If the literature departments be abolished we will soon be reaching to a total dry atmosphere, where the people will be involved in rat race of cutthroat competition. The world will be a place where language is needed for buttering, for pomp and show, and for imitation only. In one instance one may find this humankind very attractive and lucrative but the truth is that it is shallow from inside, everybody then will be leading towards a life which is a reel life & people may long for the real one.

I wish that the people dealing with literature of various languages should come in front to tell the world that science, philosophy, history, fiction etc. all are there because fiction was there in name of literature. Fiction prompted people to work on the imaginative aspect which resulted in innumerable innovations in various fields. This should give a clarion call in defense of literature. It is having the knack to change the mind.

A fable may not be doing any good to a child, but imprinting secretly on his latent mind the art of imagination. A literary work in majority makes the reader feel that the story line is quite near to his own or to the one staying next door. A feeling of closeness to the story makes an impact on mind and one comes up either with suggestions or follows the track paved by the writer.

If we search we may find that in some form or the other literature is there in our life. The initial phase of life when a child is not at all receptive to maximum things even then, lullabies sung for him (a type of oral literature) are able to make him calm. His gestures reveal that he is trying to decipher the meaning. This is an example that literature is there in the very basic lessons of life, irrespective of the caste or the status of the family. Today the people think that 'what is the need of literature'? They forget that the editorials of magazines and papers are the works of literature. Movies, plays, serials, songs all are the extended version of literature itself. What more to say all proverbs and which are having the capacity to make a tremendous change to life are the parts of famous literary works.

Nowadays the market for literary English and literature based courses is fast dwindling, paving way for Spoken English, Written English, Business English, Management English, English for IT, Technical writing, Communication Skills[4] etc. which are in great demand today. If the literary departments are closed and the knowledge of language only is imparted, we will only be producing machines and not the combination of mechanic intellect and humanitarian approach. No doubt that the above mentioned forms of English are essential to cope up with the demands of professional competition of today, but one needs a vision also to produce the best out of that knowledge. That ethical vision comes from the study of literature only.

Good books rather good literature always remains in demand. People wish to relish the cup of morning tea with newspaper, which is, if not a literature in true sense, is at least a part of it. Excellence in language can fetch one a good job, to earn luxuries for his family but then what will satisfy the inner hunger of soul? Only literature will. The number of advises we are getting from our elders are an oral version of the written literature,as all persuasive writings are having some literature as base, which gives an understanding of life,provides courage to face the challenges of life. The works of literature holds our history, our culture, our tradition, and moreover binds us with our past as well as with future. It deals with the universal problems[5] and their solutions as well.

Maxim Gorky's, "Mother" is an example of the above statement; it is portraying the conditions of the people involved and the atrocities suffered by them on the other hand. This novel must had given a lot of impetus to their contemporary struggle during October Revolution. On the same footage Indian struggle for independence was also marked with the contribution of many literary works in name of newspapers, magazines, novels etc. in absence of which we would have not been able to flourish the idea of freedom amongst the contemporary masses.

Even if one is talking purely in terms of science a deep study can confer the presence of literature at its base, though concerned with the subject only. The idea is that we have to ponder over the base of any innovation of any field. Is it not the searching of new avenues within the fold of the old researches? One can find the renowned philosophers, scientists, academicians of technical fields, judges, lawyers, financial experts, and managers are producing good literature. They supply the food which develops a strong clear, original life of the mind; which makes the imagination active and creative; which feeds the young spirit with the deeds and images of heroes; which set the real in true relations to the ideal[6].

This is like a chain,

Good literature   -   better understanding   -   new ideas   -   researches   -   new theories evolved   -   personal experiences   -   framed in literature (experiences, autobiographies)   -   good literature.

Though there is nothing in name of good or bad literature, literature is literature. But in norms of Indian ideology we are specific about judging between right and wrong according to the set prevailing norms of the society. The literary departments are just reading between the lines for the motivation of their students. In pure form of fiction also, the idea behind every plot is coming from the mind and heart which receives all the concepts from the society only. Shakespeare opened our eyes to a whole new world, peopled by the creatures of his own mind; and once we have encountered them, they seem often far more real and solid[7], his plays depict the contemporary emotions, styles, practices of the people. Canterbury Tales gives a varied picture of all the minds of different profession and age group. Tagore from India's diverse religious traditions drew many ideas, both from ancient text and popular poetry[8].

These types of works go parallel with the positive traits and flaws of the characters, through plot, and inspire the readers to go for the right path, which consists of maximum human values like honesty, dedication, truthfulness, etc. As a result these works are responsible for producing good human beings who can stand with others during their need of hour, and proving themselves the best wherever they are working.

Literature can be compared to an Ayurvedic prescription for the betterment of an individual. It cures from within turns one into a purified soul. It is not that one has to go through spiritual literature but even a simple small poem like Daffodils[9] by Wordsworth or Success/Hope[10] by Emily Dickinson, can get one connected with the natural aspect of Almighty and can reform one's individuality. It latently works for the enhancement of values in life.

Today's era require perfect balanced personalities which literature can give. Go through the life history of any of successful men and you will encounter the fact that in their young age they were introduced to good works of literature. Great literature is great only so far as it is a living organic thing, intimately related to life and related in two ways. Its tap-root lies in the soil from which it draws its sustenance; the soil of a particular age with its limitations and characteristics; but its flower is blown upon by the breezes of heaven and fed by the rain and the sun – in this respect it is related to the universal and is an expression not of an age but of ages[11].

Now a question can come that what contribution a pessimistic and bad literature can make to a person's life? Indian ideology reveals that maximum of us are taught to judge the right and wrong from our childhood days. If one is able to judge that the work is below standard or inculcating the negativity to mind; many will take the lesson not to get involved in the practices narrated in that literature. Pessimistic Shelly guides us not to become too emotional, as life is to go in all the odd situations. On the other hand write-ups of Khushwant Singh can persuade us not to go for farce.

The people, who are good, are courageous too. Literature makes one good and results in various acts even beyond capacity. Simply look into the deepness of the lines narrated by Tagore,

"Who will take my work, asks the setting sun.

None has the answer in the whole silent world.

The earthen lamp says humbly from a corner.

I will, my lord, as best as I can.[12]

It provides society with guiding principles of life. If these are not taught and plain language studies will be there, will we not be missing the emotional content from life? Electricity is having its own utility but why before every occasion traditional lamp is lighted? Because it is the base of all warmth life is having. In the same manner literature is like the foundation stones of a building, we might not be able to see them but they are there. We can ignore them for an instance but cannot remove them. Literature has always served as an authentic source of information from all around the world. Major works of history, philosophy, science, etc. are marked with the influence of literature. It serves as an enormous information base. Research works by famous inventors and literary works by notable scientists often narrate stories of their ground breaking discoveries and inferences[13].

Literature consists of the norms and rules and regulations of an idealistic society. People generally connect themselves with the characters and try to follow the idealistic track of their footprints. Human tendency is to get the appreciation and praise for each and every act of them. Literary works guide and persuade them for logical thinking about do's and don'ts which help them to come up as rational being liked by all. No scientific work can provide this service. Government now a day is working on the issues of value education through aesthetic education whereby people can learn to have the capacity to be moved by works of art, literature or music[14].

Who can ignore, "a perfect man is like a lotus - leaf in the water or like a mud - fish in the marsh"? Neither of them is polluted by the element in which it lives[15]. This comparison is only possible in literature, think who else can decipher between the lines if literary departments had not been there.

Literature brings us closer to God which indirectly purifies our soul and makes us the perfect being. The idea of direct, joyful, and totally fearless relationship with God can be found in many of Tagore's religious writings; including the poems of Gitanjali[16]. Not only this, but it can serve as a tool to combat communalism prevailing in the air of today. Tagore's devotional poems, makes them appeal to readers irrespective of their beliefs[17], the ones in particular which combine images of human love and devotion.

Every era has some needs and demands of its period. As all the fields observe change in their style and presentation so is the need of literature. Instead of eliminating it from the scene we can go for some innovative techniques of explanation; rather it can serve the purpose of interdisciplinary perspective. Literature as we have seen throughout its history, needs from time to time to be reinforced with fresh vitality, with new vigour; otherwise it will languish and decay[18].

The literature of tomorrow lies in the womb of today, every action, every attitude of ours today, is helping to mould the nature and destiny of these unborn children[19]. One should look for opportunities to showcase the power of literature, how it can evoke emotion, draw a reader into a scenario or persuade a person to change an opinion on a topic. What more to say, literature can act as[20];

- A mirror to enable readers to reflect on life problems and circumstances

- A source of knowledge

- A source of ideological challenge

- A means to keep into the past, and the future

- A means to reflect on inner struggles

- An introduction to the realities of life and death

- A vehicle for raising and discussion of social issues

Great literature is still important today. The value of reading should not be ignored even when new technologies seem to dominate our lives. Biographies inspire us to rise above our own challenges while philosophies preserved in books help us to see beyond our known boundaries. An imaginary world can give perspective by allowing us to step back and view problems in another setting. If these treasures are cast aside or replaced, our society will certainly suffer from its loss[21].

What more to say, Do you think that emotions could be felt through scientific and language subjects? True that they are there inside every human being but then who will polish them if there will be no literature teachings. It works as a sensitizing agent for heart and mind; it's like the real experience of the hardships and pleasures of life. Literature awakens, enlarges, enhances and refines our humanity in a way that almost nothing else can[22]. May be it appears as if a hyperbolic statement; but the truth is that literature gives us a style of living with all warmth of life and if it will be missing then a time will come when our world of humans be better be called as the world of Robots.

This is the high time, we need to ponder over the words of American writer James Allen, "You are today where your thoughts have brought you, and you will be tomorrow where your thoughts take you. One cannot escape the result of his thoughts"[23]. By avoiding literature we will be closing the door to a balanced life. They need to be modified to meet the demands of the age, instead of thinking about their closure, we should think for their reincarnation.

Phases of progress are known to be given by literary teachings only as the humans learn from stories[24]. All other works of science, finance, geography, computers etc. are there to result in knowledge and physical comfort; aesthetic parameter is not a part of it. On the other hand literature inculcates a perception of sensitivity, motivation and creativity. In fine we have a long way to go; in the concrete of materialism literature is like the wide shade, one should think to go with it and not without it. In the words of Frost,

"Woods are lovely dark and deep, I have promises to keep.

Miles to go before I sleep, miles to go before I sleep."[25]

It appears a bit difficult to bring the people over ethical norms but it is not impossible.

"Himalayas were once oceans and Indians once frail; a baby can come to life in test-tube and raga Malhar of Tansen could bring rain."

Nothing is impossible in this world. Nature in itself presents ample of examples which make our eyes stretch in wonder. This should act as catalyst for human beings to carry forward many impregnable tasks. Valor, caliber and determination are there to delete the word impossible form the dictionary. Dr. Kalam was once a newspaper vendor, Lal Bahadur Shasti had to cross the river currents for education; the most famous President of America Abrahim Lincon faced many failures in various arenas of his life, before becoming President. Word limit will be short if we keep on quoting the examples. It is a fact that determination and hard labor makes one excel in all norms of life.

There was a time when information was transferred manually and sometimes it was delivered, even when the significance was lost. Then time changed and the scientific advancement gifted us with cyber culture, which dissolved all the physical barriers. Today we can directly talk to the near and dear ones sitting far away with the help of web cameras. The point here is that, because the people dreamed big and acted to make them true just that is the reason behind. Why to go very far, the seven wonders of this world also indicates towards the theme.

When a baby is born who can say that the tender and fragile being, which cannot stand even is having potential of what level, but the same child can make the history too; because nothing is impossible. The journey from childhood to the old age is itself an evidence of it. Human being can not be entangled to chains. The combination of mind and heart gives a clarion call to innovations every day. From emotional sensitivity to scientific credits, economic development to cultural evolutions, nano technology to excavation of Mars every minute we are writing new definitions of success. All this is possible only because of firm devotion, it is said that we are the writer of our own destiny; we can see that the study done under the lamp post makes one a key post holder in future.

There exist some special qualities in each one of us the only need is to search and realize that, to dare for something which is revolutionary in nature and positive in effect. Many times the obstacles of life make us depressed, and we feel to give up, this is a stage when we are at the verge of losing confidence in our own self. This is the time when we have to take inspiration from the literature, successful personalities and to collect our self for hitting the target. One should not give up hope, when no task is impregnable then, why to fear in pursuing new avenues to cope up with the problems.

May be at the initial level we face some problems, our faith also will be in a trembling order but in spite of this we should not be quitters. Full determination to the given task is the best prayer to God, and can be applicable from the personal level to the level of nation and world. The concept of 'Vasudhaiv Kutumbakam' is becoming true through Globalization, science is looking after universe, medical science is taking care of body, and spiritual/sensitive literature is healing the soul. Everywhere something or the other is going on to make practical the dreams of yesterday, giving impetus to the concept of nothing is impossible.

In absence of the opportunities, our determination works, the very basic necessity water is known for its cooling effect, with constant efforts of our ancestors it is responsible for the electric power today (totally opposite to its basic nature). The key note is that that when a try is given with concrete, result oriented planning any ice can be broken, the firm devotion is the only requirement.

The famous dacoit of his times can be a saint Valmiki for the progenies, a fool Kalidas can be an immortal poet of his times, independence of India can be achieved without war, these are the examples, in which one thing is common i.e. rising against the odds, and from the opposites. Today our young generation is in grip of no. of vices, and gives the silly excuse that now we can't go back. The truth is they don't want. Even if the person is on wrong track from head to toe, law of nature says that the bright morning is always there for welcoming him rather it wishes that the will power should be collected and utilized to give up the black path.

The specialty lies in doing different things with welfare motive, to remain aloof instead of wrong company. Lotus emerges from the marsh only, but one cannot trace out even a single drop of dirt on its leaves, one has to be like this. The responsibility of future lies on this new generation, they should realize the dreams of their family and society should make themselves strong to face all hurdles and to work for innovations of various fields with ethical bent of mind. May be this appears as something beyond the average capacity but then a try has to be given, the initiative has to be taken. The famous Hindi poet Dushyant rightly said,

Kaun kahta hai aasman mein chhed nahi hota,

Ek patthar to tabiyat se ucchalon yaron.

"A book is like a garden carried in the pocket".

-Chinese proverb.

This proverb advocates the role of Literature in providing impetus to the ethical bent of mind. A garden which is having peace, serenity, piousness and happiness to serve to its visitors surely can inculcate the positivity in mind.

With the advent of human beings society took shape then there emerged the need to communicate and language came up as a result, then an indirect world of literature emerged with the imaginary power of human brain. This was a kind of parallel universe in which anything might happen and frequently did. Imagination, justice, courage, love, faith, maintaining relationships, kindness, charity, innovations, discoveries, politics, philosophy etc. are the essential entities of world. For survival we need a fit body, but for living we need to go for logical approach, a mind with sensitivity and sophistication of heart (an organ of body which runs the body and regulates the world). Phases of progress are known to be given by literary teachings only, as the humans learn from stories.

Literature is said as the mirror of society by some philosopher years back, true he was. In today's time it is not the only mirror which exposes the flaws of image, but acts as a provocateur to the reader to remove those defects, and to make the image more beautiful.

Since ages the concept of values through literature is there. Literature of each and every culture adds on lot of things to the mind. People use to develop lifelong perceptions by a simple poem or short story. As literature depicts what is going on in society, it forms a base for the progenies to frame out the sound structure of future development. It brings out the complexities of life to the sight of common masses and makes them more sensitive to the relative decisions. The morals which enter through literature leave along lasting direct/ latent impression on the minds. We can forget them for the time being but they sprout out during the need of hour as our tendency is like this. We can easily avoid the sayings and preaching's of elders, teachers and experience holders because we know them, but writer is not at all known to us and makes a psychological impact on mind. "Ghar ka jogi jogiya aan gaanv kaa siddh"

Aristotle distinguishes two kinds of virtue, one that pertains to the part of the soul that engages in reasoning (virtues of mind or intellect), and those that pertain to the part of the soul that cannot itself reason but is nonetheless capable of following reason (ethical virtues, virtues of character). Intellectual virtues are in turn divided into two sorts: those that pertain to theoretical reasoning, and those that pertain to practical thinking. He organizes his material by first studying ethical virtue in general, then moving to a discussion of particular ethical virtues (temperance, courage, and so on), and finally completing his survey by considering the intellectual virtues (practical wisdom, theoretical wisdom, etc.).

On the other hand, character ethics has nine dimensions as suggested by behavioral scientists. As under;

1. Integrity; the oneness of honest approach which cannot be disintegrated.

2. Humility; low opinion of one's importance, less proud

3. Fidelity; the faithfulness and loyalty of a person.

4. Temperance; it is the quality of self-restraint, moderation, and total abstinence from alcohol

5. Courage; it is the ability to control fear when facing danger or pain.

6. Justice; of being fair and reasonable.

7. Patience; it is the ability of calm tolerance.

8. Simplicity; quality of a person who is not showy, proud or extravagant.

9. Modesty; not behaving boastfully and avoiding indecency.

All mentioned ethics could be easily learnt through literature as it provides society with the guiding principles of life. These works make us understand the life in a better way and helps a person to take a closer look at different facets of life; it prepares the reliable foundation for self-improvement. The effort we make to enter emotionally into the higher levels of awareness experienced by saints and sages helps our creative imagination to become habituated to effect similar movements within ourselves.

Human nature is four dimensional; body, mind, heart, and spirit. In stages of development human beings found a way into the self-expression that we call literature. Our literature has much to do with life and journeys that were a constant struggle against a grim and pitiless element. Literature is where we go to explore the highest and lowest places in human society and in the human spirit, where we hope to find not absolute truth but the truth of the tale, of the imagination and of the heart. A work of literature touches the sensitivity of heart and imparts lot of belongingness towards, at times, engagements. "Live close to nature and you will never feel lonely. Don't drive those sparrows out of your veranda; they won't hack your computer".

Be it mythological literature like Ramayan & Mahabharat, or the Noble prize winning Gitanjali, be them the royal characters of Shakespeare or the common ones of R.K.Narayan all are exploring something new for every type of reader, and with it having the capacity to satisfy the mental hunger of masses and classes in moral and material terms. Literature treats all people on equal parameters without any discrimination; from streets to palaces it arouses the same emotions, only gravity may vary according to situations.

The idea of direct, joyful, and totally fearless relationship with God can be found in many of Tagore's religious writings; including the poems of Gitanjali. Additionally it serves as a tool to combat communalism prevailing in the air of today. Tagore's devotional poems, makes appeal to readers irrespective of their beliefs, particularly by those which combine images of human love and devotion.

Man's journey in this world is not merely a sum of his material needs. He has a soul, a conscience and a mind that always seek upward movement. He yearns for fulfillment, longs for love, wishes to conquer, and craves to become immortal, desires admiration and appreciation, needs emotional succor in times of distress, which administered from lowest to highest level. It makes us sophisticated beings, and refines our thoughts for leading a life of example. Literature brings us closer to God, indirectly purifies our soul to make us perfect beings. It appeals to readers irrespective of their beliefs. It awakens and enlarges, enhances and refines our humanity in a way that almost nothing else can. Literature moulds our thoughts and refines them and it makes a platform for our future. On deep scrutiny one can observe the role of emotions and feelings in life, though these are inborn traits yet it is literature which catalyzes them in right direction. Literature is an inseparable part of life, from lullabies of childhood to the movies of young age. and finally the spiritualism of old age the common is the inculcation of ethics directly or indirectly through these mediums, which are having a literature base.

Literary works go parallel with the positive traits and flaws of the characters, through plot, they inspire the readers to go for the right path, which consists of maximum human values like honesty, dedication, truthfulness, etc. As a result these works are responsible for producing good human beings who can stand with others during their need of hour, and proving themselves the best wherever they are working.

The area of literature is very wide which covers prose, poetry, drama, essays, fiction, philosophy, art, history, religion, culture, science, and legal writings. It lays the foundation of an enriched life and adds life to living. Reading literature is not only a matter of taste and intelligence, it is a matter of character as well.

Literature inculcates a positive attitude and instigates WILL to concentrate on the work to achieve greater heights. "When pain ends, gain ends too" is the true assessment made by Robert browning.

Cowards die many times before their deaths; the valiant never taste of death but once.

and

"One impulse from a vernal wood

May teach you more of man,

Of moral evil and of good,

Than all the ages can."

These lines comprise of few words only but give the deep philosophy of life in name of ethics.

Every era has some needs and demands. As all the fields observe change in their style and presentation so is the need of literature, some innovative techniques of explanation; interdisciplinary perspective, should be adopted to mark its relevance to the contemporary world. Every concept needs from time to time to be reinforced with fresh vitality, with new vigour; otherwise it will languish and decay.

Governments these days are working on the issues of value education through aesthetic education whereby people can learn to have the capacity to be moved by works of art, literature or music. This step itself makes clear the relevance of art and literature in the world. Literature is treading towards a new set up. Like preceding works it is not only revealing the problems flowing undercurrent but giving a solution for the eradication of those evils. Literature inculcates a sort of courage, and the mind takes the right decision. It can be said that many writers and poets knowingly or unknowingly give a glimpse of social evils, criticize them and by the end of the work provide solutions to the reader to remove them from society.

Though there is no guarantee that the solution given by them in general is applicable to the practical life too, but in specific, as the plot comes from society, it could be said that, literature is a platform where many could find a solution to their problems. It serves as a social reformer and helps out in eradication of social evils if not in totality then in partial at least. Today we need to nurture the ethics in our progenies through literature as its prominent feature is that it is having something for each and every strata of society inclusive of politicians, sociologists, historians, economists, scholars, scientists, workers, industrialists, and common masses as well.

Literature consists of the norms and rules and regulations of an idealistic society. People generally connect themselves with the characters and try to follow the idealistic track of their footprints. Through stories and poems people connect themselves to the life and find to trace out the hidden solution in these literary works. And above all, it stimulates the reader to think about the perennial questions of ethics. "Pride engraves his frowns in stones; love offers her surrender in flowers". In fine we can say that literature is having the capacity to rectify even the worst mistakes of your life. It always suggests some way out to deal with obstacles in an ethical manner. To sum up it could be said that literature is just like the profound poem of Emily Dikinson,

"Hope is the thing with feathers

That perches in the soul.

And sings the tune

Without the words,

and never stops at all."

"Every child comes with the message that God is not yet discouraged of man." In other words still the air is having fragrance of ethics through the flowers of faith bored by the deep rooted values.

Imagination, justice, courage, love, faith, maintaining relationships, kindness, charity, innovations, discoveries, politics, philosophy etc. are the essential entities of world. And when we talk of world the mention of nature, society, human beings is there. For survival we need a fit body, but for living we need to go for logical approach, a mind with sensitivity and sophistication of heart (an organ of body which runs the body and regulates the world). Phases of progress are known to be given by literary teachings only, as the humans learn from stories.

On deep scrutinizing one could observe the role of emotions and feelings in life, though these are inborn traits yet there is something which catalyze them and that is literature. Literature is an inseparable part of life, from lullabies of childhood to the movies of young age and finally the spiritualism of old age the common is the inculcation of ethics directly or indirectly through these mediums, which are having a literature base.

The modern era of today is the era of cut throat competitions and head to toe materialism, but still for living a life we need ethics and moral values, since ages literature is providing this service to the mankind. It comes from society itself and acts as a mirror too. It is ethical because it dares to expose the rotten customs, in-just rules and atrocities of masses and vices of classes. Various classics are the examples. A question can emerge that if it only exposes the under current how it can be ethical? The answer is, many sufferers get the solution to their sufferings, many gets motivation to clean the system, and many from the capable section try to reform the system. In a nutshell the topic lines of a literary work are having the capacity to persuade the people more as compared to any other means.

"If I can stop one heart from breaking, I shall not live in vain."

The morals which enter through literature and culture leave a long lasting latent impression on the minds. May be we can forget them for the time being but they sprout out during the need of hour as the tendency of us is like this. We can easily avoid the sayings and preaching of elders, teachers and the experience holders because we know them, but a writer is not at all known to us and that makes a psychological impact on the mind.

We should always remember that the height of building we see is only the visible half. The great monuments which are there for hundreds of years are due to the bottom half of their strong foundation. In life this foundation of ethics is having the firm concrete grip of literary cement.

"Poetry is the first and last of all knowledge - it is as immortal as the heart of man."

The roots below the earth claim no reward for making the branches fruitful, same is there with literature it seeks no recognition for imbibing morals and values to our life. It works for enhancing our courage, love, faith, imagination, relationships etc. Not only this it expands and explores new definitions of them with every new work of literature. Our independence and the revolutions worldwide are there because mention of problems related to them was there in the contemporary literature.

These lines are good enough to make you realize that the reality of keeping feet at ground is always good. Literature introduces us to a new world of experience, we grow and emerge through literature, and as it is related to thought it is universal. Rather it is an inseparable part of our lives, since child hood we are more receptive to the world of fairy tales and fiction. Literature takes care of all the aspects of life, it is a true guide and guide can never be unethical, during time of stress it relaxes and suggests solution. Through the characters of literary works we used to get motivation and inspiration. Writer discovers a story when a personality passes through a crisis of spirit or circumstances; character either resolves it or lives with it.

Today we need to nurture the ethics of our progenies through literature as its prominent feature is that it is having something for each and every strata of society inclusive of politicians, sociologists, historians, economists, scholars, scientists, workers, industrialists, and common masses as well.

Be it mythological literature like Ramayan & Mahabharat, or the Noble prize winning Gitanjali, be them the royal characters of Shakespeare or the common ones of R.K.Narayan all are exploring something new for every type of reader, and with it having the capacity to satisfy the mental hunger from masses to classes in terms on morality and of materialism too. Literature treats all people on equal parameters without any discrimination; from streets to palaces it arouses the same emotions, only gravity of them can change according to situations.

Literature brings us closer to God which indirectly purifies our soul to make us perfect beings. It appeals to readers irrespective of their beliefs. It awakens and enlarges, enhances and refines our humanity in a way that almost nothing else can. Literature moulds our thoughts and refines them and it makes a platform for our future.

Man's journey in this world is not merely a sum of his material needs. He has a soul, a conscience and a mind that always seek upward movement. He yearns for fulfillment, longs for love, wishes to conquer, and craves to become immortal, desires admiration and appreciation, needs emotional succor in times of distress, which are not given by the literature but its base, is prepared by it only. It makes us sophisticated beings, and refines our thoughts for leading a life of example.

In today's busy lifestyle we hardly have any time to give special time to literature but as it has discussed earlier it is there in movies, serials, newspapers, proverbs and in advices, we can easily go through even in rush of life. Even if we talk about farce, or the type which glamorize the wrong side of society or gives more weightage to wrong practices in name of time or modernization is providing guidance by opening our eyes to the vices of surroundings. In general people of all religion and of every nook and corner of the world hold a clear perception about right and wrong, dos' and dons'. So in a way it highlights the reality of behind the curtains, i.e. an indirect message to be ethical, it gives a picture of the after effects of wrong deeds.

A book can be moral if it raises moral questions even if it doesn't provide moral answers. This way we can say that it acts as the firm and static foundation of life. Some traits it gives directly and some are instilled indirectly. Though the changing trend of education is having very less exposure to this medium of ethics. We should ponder over this in a serious manner and should utilize its interdisciplinary approach for the upbringing of our progenies.

References:

1. Krishnaswamy N & Krishnaswamy Lalitha,The Story of English Language in India, Foundation Books, New Delhi, 2006, p-39

2. ibid, p-127

3. Rikett Arthur Comton, A History of English Literature, USB Pub. & Dis. Pvt. Ltd., New Delhi, 2006, p- 659

4. Krishnaswamy N & Krishnaswamy Lalitha,The Story of English Language in India, Foundation Books, New Delhi, 2006, p-181,

5. Rikett Arthur Comton, A History of English Literature USB Pub. & Dis. Pvt. Ltd., New Delhi, 2006, p- 664

6. Source; Internet

7. Quennell Peter & Johnson Hamish, Who's Who in Shakespeare, Routledge, London, preface-viii

8. Sen Amartya, The Argumentative Indians, Penguin Books, London,2005, p- 96

9. Wordsworth William, Poems in two Volumes, Vol.1, Longman, London, 1807.

10. Dickinson Emily, The Collected Poems of Emily Dickinson, Barnes & Noble Books, New York,2003, p – 6 & 22

11. Rikett Arthur Comton, A History of English Literature, USB Pub. & Dis. Pvt. Ltd., New Delhi, 2006, p- 664

12. Tagore Rabindranath, Ref; Competition Science Vision, Mar2000, p-5

13. Oak Manali, Importance of Literature, on Internet.

14. Aspin N. David & Chapman D.Judith, Value Education and Lifelong Learning, Springer, The Netherlands, 2007, p-22

15. Muller Max, Ramkrishna, His Life and Sayings, p- 112

16. Sen Amartya, The Argumentative Indians, Penguin Books, London,2005, p-96

17. Radice William, Rabindranath Tagore; Selected Short Stories, Harmonds worth; Penguine, 1991, p – 28

18. Rikett Arthur Comton, A History of English Literature, USB Pub. & Dis. Pvt. Ltd., New Delhi, 2006, p – 659

19. Ibid, p – 680

20. Cairney Trevor H., Pathways to Literacy, Cassell, London, 1995, p – 77,78.

21. Timson Levi, The Relevance of Literature, source; Internet

22. Gioia Diana, Importance of Reading, The Commonwealth June 2006, in National Endowments for the Arts, p – 19

23. Giardina Ric, Living a Balanced Life, Infinity Books, New Delhi, 2005, p-29

24. Aspin N. David & Chapman D. Judith (Editors), Value Education and Lifelong Learning, Springer, The Netherlands, 2007, p-140

25. Frost Robert "Stopping by Woods on a Snowy Evening" is a poem written in 1922, published in 1923 in his New Hampshire volume

26. Aspin N. David & Chapman D.Judith, Value Education and Lifelong Learning, Springer, The Netherlands, 2007,

27. Cairney Trevor H., Pathways to Literacy, Cassell, London, 1995.

28. Dickinson Emily, The Collected Poems of Emily Dickinson, Barnes & Noble Books, New York,2003,

29. Frost Robert "Stopping by Woods on a Snowy Evening" is a poem written in 1922, published in 1923 in his New Hampshire volume.

30. Giardina Ric, Living a Balanced Life, Infinity Books, New Delhi, 2005.

31. Gioia Diana, Importance of Reading, The Commonwealth June 2006, in National Endowments for the Arts.

32. Krishnaswamy N & Krishnaswamy Lalitha,The Story of English Language in India, Foundation Books, New Delhi, 2006,

33. Muller Max, Ramkrishna, His Life and Sayings,

34. Oak Manali, Importance of Literature, on Internet.

35. Quennell Peter & Johnson Hamish, Who's Who in Shakespeare, Routledge, London, preface-viii

36. Radice William, Rabindranath Tagore; Selected Short Stories, Harmonds worth; Penguine, 1991.

37. Rikett Arthur Comton, A History of English Literature, USB Pub. & Dis. Pvt. Ltd., New Delhi, 2006,

38. Sen Amartya, The Argumentative Indians, Penguin Books, London,2005,

39. Source; Internet

40. Tagore Rabindranath, Ref; Competition Science Vision, Mar2000, p-5

41. Timson Levi, The Relevance of Literature, source; Internet

42. Wordsworth William, Poems in two Volumes, Vol.1, Longman, London, 1807.

Chapter 5

Suppositions

Though it is difficult to come up with some conclusion on such a vast topic of ethics, but every work has to be accomplished for the society and progenies to take benefit. The observation says that the world is ruled by the wisdom not by the weapon. Modification of society to a peaceful place of living has to be the objective of all. But as this is not there, we need such type of works, which can tell us the importance of values in life with the materialism.

Wisdom certainly imposes restrictions on wild behavior of human beings. We are concerned with the essential worth of the reasoning or logical calculations that compel us to impose them. Finer sentiments can never take root in our personality as long as we wish to entertain them only for a diplomatic handling of the situations external to us. As each one of us is guided by a selective impulse from inside, a comparative study of the various systems is bound to evoke a natural response from within. It helps us in choosing, a system which suits our temperament. Then we make a wise approach to philosophy itself, instead of allowing the structure of each system to remain apart pointing to a path lightening intellectual conclusions at its top. We propose to traverse the steps, take the torch and introduce it into all the intricate movements of life, as we live it, verifying its lightening power as we proceed.

Then our emotional awareness of what we call love, goodwill, beauty, prayer, peace, prosperity and so on can be established on sublime levels and raised to such intensity that it can penetrate egoistic walls and take the advantage of transmission. Generations of earnest people from all walks of life, have been engaged in perfecting themselves and accumulating creative energy. This inner virtue got by the fusion of mastered values, that has become expressed not only as the well-known religious movements of the present day, but also as the spirit of dedication behind the advances made in almost every field of human activity.

In life we need a teacher who can guide us for the illuminated path, without a living teacher as a standard of reference, we are likely to miss the true implications of the technical terms of the different systems, and move our internal limbs in most unprofitable if not in harmful ways. The culture, aesthetic values etc. can catalyze such principles to life, i.e. they can play the role of a teacher. Literature thus can become a vision that supplements and balances the parameters of life.

Progress and success whether individual or collective, depends upon our learning to react promptly and in ways that draw out and coordinate the virtues present in every context. Spirituality, philosophy, culture etc. are at their best, the disciplines to help us learn this supreme art of being ethical and making ethical.

Human nature is full of possibilities, only a small fraction of it is turned into actualities. Every forward step is taken by men who are passionately devoted to truth, have unshakable faith and have value implementation. The instrument for instilling the spirit of coordination has been oral tradition containing stories and parables. They were set for the inner refinement. Literature, art, social customs, festivals etc. help in the realization of the cosmic or divine element in the human personality. They are there to constitute a mental useful storehouse from which useful suggestions for day to day conduct might be freely drawn in future. We need to ponder over this art of incorporating morals and values to life.

There is a need to provide a positive atmosphere to the lifestyle. Ramkrishna opined that "Mind is everything. If mind loses its liberty you lose yours. If the mind is free, you are free too. The mind can be dipped in any colour, like a white cloth. If the mind be kept in bad company, it will colour one's thought and conversation. Placed in the midst of devotees, it can meditate on God as well. It changes its nature according to the things amongst which it lives and acts." We thus need a platform where we can provide a positive nurturing to our mind.

No doubt a proper training is needed for all this. It is said that a successful teacher is the one who takes note of every factor and gently puts in a word here and an explanation there in midst of casual talks. And if he succeeds in helping his students to get a better perspective, they will alter their conduct of their own accord in due course. And that's how he knows to present the lives of eminent men and women to his students in such ways as to stimulate their imagination and make them frame heroic ideals suited to their inborn tastes. That teacher alone serves most that discerns the total range of student's personality and emotionally plants him at its very center. What happens is that in most of the cases that the mind of serving person is not thoroughly purified. At times he entertains the feelings of suspicion, enmity etc. towards other leaders in the field whom he regards as his rival, that way attractive power of the love is nullified by the opposing pulls of base emotions. There we need the ethical bent of mind, which without prejudice can not only teach but preach as well.

Encouragement is a miracle, it can be instilled to the minds and a great change can be observed. At the initial stage this may not sound as very convincing note but slowly and steadily it could be understood and will be able to create wonders. Law of nature says, 'to err is human', positivity of life lies in learning from errors towards improvement. One should not be criticized only for mistakes rather some suggestions with the flavor of concern should be implied. Repeated criticism will not only antagonize the other party but will destroy all the scope to improve. Contrary to this support and encouragement can bring wonderful results. It is always important to show pleasure, friendliness, admiration, respect, regard, curiosity, and wiliness to help when you meet the fellow in this regard, as these are also the means to make one ethical.

The surrounding people in name of family, relatives and friends need not to be criticized and compared unfavorably, instead notice and highlight even the smallest improvements and targets achieved by them. Spur others to great success and achievements, now you can observe the automatic success of yours in gaining leadership, respect and love over the people whom you need to govern. Pursuing the subordinates for 'never give up' stand despite their trials, tribulations, setbacks, illness etc. Ask them for perseverance, devotion and one point dedication to hit the target of life.

We do have Government, NGOs, Social societies, Educational Institutes, and above all a family system yet if we look at the moral condition of society it is pathetic. Various vices are still there hindering the ethical society. This work is an effort to avail the benefits of piousness, an effort to suggest that a practical means of avoiding the hostile dichotomy between law and ethics is to use it as a teaching tool, integrated into every area of the curriculum.

We need to discern that law and social restrictions come at the secondary stage, so why not to nip into the bud at the primary stage only. Why not to start from the very nitty-gritties of life but not in form of moral studies only but to give the young minds a practical insertion to the efficacy of values in life.

The aim is to come up with an environment where we need not to talk about natural or legal justice but it comes automatically to us. Ethics is the only parameter which can facilitate society with a world which is beautiful in is true nature and not for the purpose of showcasing only.

The battle of life is nothing but the survival of the fittest, both physical and more importantly psychological. We only require will power for many things in life, through galvanization and motivation we can bring a person back to life which is a service to humanity. In fine, we need to support people with,

"He wins the most that can endure the most, faces issues, never shirks, and always works. He alone is great who by life heroic, conquers fate. Adversity is the prosperity of the great. Kites rise against, not with the wind."